# DEDICATION

*This book is humbly dedicated to the walking wounded.*
*To you, my deepest apologies.*
*Not only for my own failings, but on behalf of every person*
*who misrepresented the Truth when you needed it most;*
*Please forgive us.*

WHEN THE END OF THE ROAD
IS JUST THE BEGINNING.

# Meeting God
# THE
# HARD
# WAY

TERI BRINSLEY

# Meeting God THE HARD WAY

ISBN Number: 979-8-9868281-0-7

# ACKNOWLEDGEMENTS

*Writing a book like this has been a labor of love not only on my part, but also for several others who've helped me along the way.*

*Thank you to those of you who have encouraged my vision to write this book.*

*First and foremost to my immediate family: My husband David, and my kids, Shelbie, Daryl, Kristen, Jake, Zach, Nicolas and Bailey. Each of you have encouraged me throughout the entire process of seeing this book through to the end. Thank you for being gracious and forgiving those moments I've been cranky or when I've missed time with you because I was writing. Thank you, David, for allowing me to share some of our very personal stories and for always being willing to patiently listen over and over as I'd read each completed chapter to you. You helped me hammer out just the right words when I'd get stuck. And to Zach, I appreciate your patient help on this beautiful book cover. This book wouldn't be what it is without each of you.*

*Thank you to Aunt Glenda and to Zula for reminding me that this book was already written inside me and had been merely waiting for me to put it onto paper. Thank you for encouraging me every step of the way and gently nudging me to keep going those times I wanted to quit.*

*Thank you to Sue Sundstrom, my literal God-send writing coach for your creative wisdom shared. By following your lead through the process of writing, formatting and publishing, you've greatly helped to make this book a reality (and became a special friend along the way!) And to Candice Mitchell, editor extraordinaire: you seemed to effortlessly understand my writing style. What a huge help you've been. You've both raised the bar of my writing to a new level. I'm so thankful our paths have crossed.*

*Thank you to the precious friends and extended family members who've cheered me on and allowed me to send you very rough draft paragraphs for feedback. You gave me your honest thoughts which I valued very much. I've taken to heart each and every comment you took of your time to share and have lovingly woven some among the words of this book.*

*To my brother, Tim, the one who shared my childhood. I've never known a day on the planet without you. You were a strong anchor that steadied me while we were growing up (and sometimes still are.) Thanks for loving me. I was then, I am now, and will always be so very grateful for you.*

# Contents

Dedication ..................................................................iii

Acknowledgements ...................................................... v

Introduction .............................................................. 1

Chapter 1: Meeting God in the Chair of a Child ........................... 7

Chapter 2: Meeting God Before Time.................................25

Chapter 3: Meeting God in My Shame ........................ 43

Chapter 4: Meeting God at Sunset ............................57

Chapter 5: Meeting God in my Fear.............................75

Chapter 6: Meeting God in the Bathroom....................95

Chapter 7: Meeting God in my Sadness.................... 113

Chapter 8: Meeting God in My Rejection.................. 127

Chapter 9: Meeting God in the Grocery Store ........... 143

Chapter 10: Meeting God in My Choices ................... 159

Chapter 11: Meeting God in My Words..................... 175

Chapter 12: Meeting God in My Mama ..................... 191

Conclusion: Meeting God in Your Story ....................213

Bonus Feature.............................................................223

About the Author.........................................................226

I'm like a singer, guitar in hand
standing on an overpass at rush hour.
I'm belting out my song
as the cars rush past.
If you happen to be driving by
with your windows down
perhaps you'll catch a faint melody…

I hope it reminds you of
a song all your own.
May you begin humming a tune
picking up the words
as you drive along.

*Teri Brinsley*

# INTRODUCTION

Is God a No-Show?

Whatever led you to this moment and the desire to glance at this book, I want you to know up front, your doubts are completely safe here. In fact, they are welcome.

I believe it's healthy and responsible to raise an eyebrow when approaching such an ominous topic. I, too, have been skeptical when reading what others have to say on the subject of God. It's why writing this particular book has been the most daunting task I've ever taken on. Still, I felt the incessant draw to spill pieces of my heart onto paper. This is my story. My experience that I share. It is not coming from a know-it-all position. Far from it. With each page I've written, and as my life stories are retold, a realization grows in me of how very much more there is to learn. I've but scratched the surface.

In the hard as well as the blissful seasons of my life, what I've personally experienced steadily convinces me more and more of the undeniable, unshakable Truth (with a capital T): *God most definitely exists and He cares for us more than I could ever fathom.* I've just had difficulty wrapping my head around that Truth at times.

These true-life stories may seem trivial to some, and that's okay. They're not for everyone. I risk sharing them anyway. I write this for those who, despite all their searching, still find themselves wrestling with unanswerable burnings in their soul. For the ones, like me, who've been abused by cold, hard religion and disillusioned by the blatant hypocrisy therein; for those whose trust was met with lies, we are the ones who've spit out the canned versions, refusing to swallow what we've been spoon-fed.

Between these pages, I hope I've created a gentle space to breathe. This is a place where we can talk about such things without fear and without judgment.

Together, we'll face questions like:

> *"Does God really exist?"*
> *"Does God even care about what I'm going through?"*
> *"Is God mad at me?"*
> *"If He does exist, where has He been?"*
> *"Is God a no-show?"*

Deep down most of us believe in God, even if we don't know how to articulate it. We might not readily admit it aloud, but we innately crave a *firsthand* experience with our Creator. It's all the religious mumbo jumbo that we often have difficulty with. If only we could cut through all that and simply get to *Him*. Having our own personal connection would surely help clear things up. We've heard the stories others tell. Though it can shed a flickering light, someone else's experience, or knowledge of God, doesn't really cut it. We want to know, feel, *experience Him* for ourselves. Despite all we've been through, we still carry the faint hope for an undeniable encounter with this Eternal Father Being.

Allowing ourselves to acknowledge this is not without risk. Entertaining thoughts of personally connecting with the Almighty can make us feel childishly silly. Like waking up early on Christmas morning, hoping to catch a glimpse of the jolly man in red velvet only to find mom in her bathrobe slipping gifts in our stockings. Feeling foolish for such a naive belief could be the reason we shove down thoughts like this and never ever face them. We don't want to be that vulnerable. We can't risk Him not showing up, then experience the feeling of stupidity for believing in the first place.

But still, the draw lingers... it remains. At desperate times it surfaces. Some of us do come to Him heart in hand. We have a threatening situation, a life-altering decision to make, and we truly need holy discernment at the crossroads. So, we hold it all up to Him for clarity. But often, we're met with nothing more than a deafening silence. When the fog clears, our disappointment turns to anger. *Where was He? He could have done something but didn't! Doesn't He care? How could He leave me alone in this?*

So where do we go from here?

We should probably start with asking ourselves this basic question: "Who is this God I'm praying to?" If we aren't careful, avoiding this step could become the very roadblock that keeps us from ever moving forward in our faith.

**Don't be afraid to ask this question.** Without bravely asking, you'll never know the answer. And isn't that the whole point?

Everywhere we turn, we see an array of religions offering us a smorgasbord of god identities—each one clashing with the next. Who's the real deal? Which is the "true" god? Aren't they all just pieces of a whole? How can we know for sure? How do we choose what to believe?

Where does God reside? How can I meet someone I can never find? Why is He such a paradox? How are we supposed to relate to a God we can't communicate with? Why continue seeking and praying only to receive what feels like continual almighty rejection? Feeling ignored by the Creator of the Universe is the ultimate feeling of rejection. It can suck the faith right out of us. And often does. It feels cruel and so very confusing.

With so much clamoring, who can we trust to tell us *the truth about God?* What if the *reason* we keep being disappointed isn't what we think it is? What if it's as simple as considering that maybe we've been viewing God all wrong? What if our focus simply needs a slight adjustment and our ears only need a bit of fine-tuning?

Are you brave enough to ask yourself these questions?

I challenge you to be brave. Read the book. Ponder the questions at the end of each chapter and journal your answers *honestly.* Take the time to reflect on what you've written and—dare I say it—pray. *Then*, decide for yourself.

The brave one, the wise one, is NOT the one who's so steadfast in their own opinions that they smugly dismiss another's point of view by quickly reciting their own. On the contrary, it's the one who's willing to listen. It's the one who's stomach churns as they begin to understand their own imperfectly limited humanness, acknowledging they have room to grow. Standing to face all they've held as truth; they willingly allow it to be shaken. The one who doesn't turn away as these beliefs are challenged, is the brave soul. In this moment, their bravery comes not from their own reasoning, but because they risk standing on something greater than themselves.

If God personally whispered in your ear or mine, would we recognize His voice? The Bible does say He's been speaking for all of eternity. Why, then, has it been so hard to hear Him?

What I can tell you is this: I know both you and I are equally able to hear Him when He speaks. Yes, you can meet God. Chances are, you already have—you just didn't recognize Him. How can I say this? Because there were many times in my own life when I didn't recognize Him, I thought I was alone. It would be later, looking back, when I would learn that He most certainly was there. And He doesn't play favorites. If He's been there with me, for me, whether I knew it or not—He's certainly doing the same for you.

Yes, I've met God many times. And each time, I have found myself permanently altered—changed for the better somehow. Meeting Him seldom happens the way I think it will. My encounters rarely occur on shining mountaintops when life is going great. No, not at all. It's usually in my darkest moments, in my deepest disappointments and sharpest pain—in my wreckage—He meets me. When I've screwed things up beyond repair… that seems to be His favorite time to connect.

For me, meeting God seems to come *the hard way.*

# Chapter 1

# MEETING GOD IN THE CHAIR OF A CHILD

y stomach did double flips as I climbed the stairs toward her office. It felt like showing up for an elective root canal. What was I thinking when I scheduled this first appointment with a therapist? Bearing one's soul to some stranger sounded less appealing than a jab of Novocain and the yanking of a tooth. I cringed at the thought of it. It was clear to me I would need to cling to what little courage I had just to get through what I'd started here. Bravely, I reached for the knob and turned it. I knew there was no going back.

The feel of the room was foreign—almost clammy. Or was that just me? Why didn't they at least take the time to make this awkward environment a little more welcoming for us train wrecks? Maybe a little candle on a shelf? The gentle flickering with a fake scent of baked cookies or something would've been nice. Any resemblance of comfort would've been much appreciated.

With a surrendering sigh, I took my seat in the empty chair closest to the door. It was an easy exit if I changed my mind. I noticed a man sitting there, pretending not to notice me. In my timid entrance, he'd never looked up. Remaining deathly still, his nose never left position, steadily pointing downward between the pages of his hardcover book. I didn't bring a book. Smartphones weren't a thing yet, so there would be no scrolling screen of distraction either. Instead, glancing around the room for something of interest, I did my best to get my mind off what was coming.

Noting a silk flower arrangement in the corner, I gave it more attention than it asked for. I pondered how long the poor thing had been sitting there. Its colors were muted, appearing to have faded with time. How did it end up as a subpar décor piece in this lifeless room? Had it spent its whole sad life sitting there collecting dust on that stoic little table? With nothing else to do, I considered scenarios.

Perhaps its flowers were brighter at one time. It was hard to tell by looking at it now. Maybe, it was once a gift given to someone special. It was most likely nothing more than a discounted clearance item. Something no shopper wanted, except the one who took pity on it, given its current purpose. It had been, at least for now, spared the fate of a garbage can. I felt a lot like that flower arrangement.

There were a few outdated magazines scattered atop a small oval table that was too far to reach without getting up. Though mildly tempting, I left them as they lay. The last thing I was going to do was to draw further attention to myself. In this arena, the goal was to be as invisible as possible. I would not allow the chance of making eye contact with that other poor soul while we both waited to be verbally fileted. We never nodded or spoke, yet suddenly, a strange comfort arose as I realized this one thing we shared in common— our vulnerability of the moment. I settled into my chair with that thought.

Finally, the door to her office swung open and two women emerged. My heart momentarily jumped into my throat, blocking my ability to breathe. I instinctively lowered my gaze as to give some sort of privacy to the lady whose appointment had just ended. I maintained a steadfast interest in the waiting room carpet, until I could stand it no longer. The sniffles from this teary-eyed woman had pulled my curiosity upward. In short secretive glances, my eyes followed her as together they moved closer toward the exit. The woman dabbed her eyes with a tissue as the counselor gave her a professional pat on the back and the light reassurance that she'd *see her next week*. The woman nodded, dropping her view to the very same carpet I had found less than inspiring. *I get it. There's no eye contact in this place. I feel you, sister.* I kept my condolences to myself. She shuffled past me, just missing the edge of my knees, and was gone. How would she face the rest of her day? Would she be okay? A tug of sadness, concern for this stranger, came over me. The way her shoulders sank, seeming so heavy as she passed by, left a weight in me too. She looked as though she'd been carrying her entire world on that narrow frame. My view of her also made me shudder, as I considered how others might judge my appearance when I would exit…

"Teri?" The counselor broke into my empathetic thoughts. She was now looking directly at me, gesturing with her hand. "Please come in and make yourself comfortable."

I tossed back an acknowledgement, "Sure!" at the same time internally snarking what I really wanted to say, *Make myself comfortable? Yeahhhh, like that's an option!?* I obediently rose and joined her as she ushered me into the dreaded room. As if it were made of steel from a dungeon, the door closed and latched behind us. I stifled the very real urge to run.

At the onset of that first visit, I remember asking her right up front how many sessions she thought it would take to get me "fixed." It's almost comical to recall how at the time I honestly believed what was going on in me could be fixed or at least managed with a few bullet points on a handy tear sheet.

Instead of answering my initial question, she redirected it, spinning me into the position of answering all of hers. The minutes of that first meeting painfully ticked by as, one after the next, my parrot-like responses met her seemingly endless trail of asks. This nonsense filled our high-priced time together. Her line of questioning was obvious, all of it mindlessly trivial to me…

"I see from your file you're married?"

"How many years?

"That's great!"

"And kids?"

"Four, is it? Wow!"

"That's impressive."

"What are your kid's names?"

"How old? You've got some spacing in there. Good for you."

"Do you enjoy being a mom? I'll bet it's challenging with four!"

"And you work outside the home also?"

"Tell me more about that."

"What's your favorite thing about your job?"

"I'll bet it's challenging. Do you enjoy it?"

"That sounds so interesting!"

Surface social chit chat at a hundred dollars per hour, I wasn't digging it. *Why all the superficial questions? We aren't going to be girlfriends. This isn't a sleepover where we share stories and braid each other's hair. I don't have time for this ridiculousness and certainly not the money! Can we please just cut to the chase and get to the point?* My foggy-eyed stare, or the borderline rudeness in my curt answers, must have given away my internal dialogue.

Adjusting her glasses, she narrowed her gaze to look me squarely in the eye. She was politely serious, like a white-coated scientist examining a lab rat.

"Okay… let's move into talking a little bit about why you've come to see me today. Can you share what's currently going on? What is it that brought you here?"

Begging for first dibs at this one, my inner voice was jumping up and down in my head, *"Well Doc, If I knew why, I wouldn't be here! I wouldn't need YOU, would I?!"* Quickly shoving my smart aleck thoughts aside, I cleared my throat attempting to give her a reasonable answer, "Ummmm… no. I can't really tell you why I'm here other than the fact that I keep having some sort of panic attacks. My life seems… well, out of control somehow? All I know is that I can't go on like this, so I decided to come see you."

My mind trailed on; *That was definitely harder to say than I thought it would be… But hey, I did it! I gave you what you wanted. Now it's your turn. I'm ready for those bullet points, lady. Just lay 'em on me and I'll get to work! Whatcha got for me? Five steps to kick anxiety? Seven secrets to conquering my fears? Something like that? Whatever it takes. I'm ready! Hit me with it!*

Let's just say that I got no bullet points. No lists. Not even a single pre-printed take home sheet. Instead, somewhere between that appointment and the many that would come after it, her persistent digging would finally strike a vein. As she'd continue to swing that pickaxe, something deep in my soul was slowly giving way. My confidence in my own abilities to manage whatever the problem might be, would be shaken to its core and I was far from prepared for that. I had no clue what would soon come spilling out of my own mouth, but I would put up a fight before we got to that point!

"Let's talk just a little bit about your childhood, Teri." Her irritating question filled the air like an ominous black cloud. There was no way to escape, but I needed to try.

"What did you say?" I choked out an almost laughing reply. "Are you serious? Come on. Are you really asking me about my childhood stuff?" My thoughts objected, *Oh, no thank you. This is ridiculous and not going to happen. Talking about my childhood? How cheesy can you get?*

I straightened my back tall into her scratchily woven not-fooling-anybody therapist couch. It was time for a quick reset with this woman. "Didn't I make it clear? I'm here to move forward—not to take a mental stroll down the streets of my childhood." Flashing a smile in a futile attempt to soften the blow of what I'd just said, I articulated my genuine thoughts further. Speaking my words slowly, I hoped to be clearly understood this time, "I'm sorry. What I mean is… It's just that…Well, no offense, but talking about my childhood as some sort of therapy seems sooo cliché!" I didn't want to disrespect her guidance, but this wasn't going to happen. It was a big fat no.

My attempt at politeness didn't fool her. Nor did it distract her from the direction at hand. She continued to look me straight in the eye, not saying a word.

Uncomfortable with the silence of this professionally intrusive stranger, I took the opportunity to fill the audible space, "I don't see how talking about my life as a little kid has any relevance to what's happening in my life currently. Really! What I mean is, doesn't everybody have a sad story they could dig up from their childhood? A recounting of wrongs? A heartbreaking list of broken dreams? That's just life! I've dealt with mine. I'm good!"

This time she replied with an almost stern directness, "I want to hear about yours. I think it's important."

Wow! Could she tell that she'd just mentally ninja punched me, kicking my mind into high gear? My head was aching. We'd barely begun this session and I was ready to grab my coat. My irritation with her at this point was only surpassed by my concern for what she'd think of my rudeness if I simply got up and walked out. If I couldn't leave physically, I might as well stay fully engaged and drive my point home.

"Look. We all have our stories, don't we? How is my childhood any different from those of a million others? I just don't see the need to spend this time (and money I don't have) revisiting the unfortunate moments of my young life. It's in the past and that's exactly where it should stay. Talking about it, reliving it, wouldn't change a thing. History can't be rewritten, so why drudge it up?"

I continued, "I know people with much worse stories than mine, and they're doing just fine as adults. And so am I. I choose to focus on what I can do today to make my life better. I don't sit and wallow in the past. I'm not a poor child victim. I'm a responsible, grown adult. I've pulled myself up by my own bootstraps and moved forward... and I'm proud of it!"

Pausing only to take a breath, I concluded, "Blame doesn't work for me. Finger-pointing is incredibly weak. It's a victim's way out, a way of avoiding taking control of their own life. I take responsibility for myself. I work hard to have the life and relationships I have. We all have choices, don't we? Getting into all that 'woe is me, my life has been so hard' stuff leads nowhere. Now, please...can we move on?" I ended my rant hoping to make my position heard loud and clear.

Barely blinking at my lengthy tirade, she tilted her head slightly to one side and simply responded, "So, why *are* you here?"

I was speechless.

For a moment it felt as if all the air had been sucked from the room, but somehow, I was still breathing. Well played, counselor. Well played. She might as well have said, "Check mate."

We sat in uncomfortable silence, her staring at me, and me staring at anything other than her. In recollection, this silence lasted the rest of that visit.

I wasn't sure there would be a next one. Until there was.

I'm not sure how, but slowly over the course of many visits, together we began gently unpacking the layers of my history. At first, sorting out memories from my childhood seemed tedious. I'd neatly folded and put away so many things already, why were we now dragging them back out again? I'd wrongly assumed I'd already cleaned up all those messes in my life. But, eventually as the childhood thread continued to be tugged at, suddenly, in an instant it happened. We hit the motherload. Now, it was time to deal with what I never knew was there.

Maybe it shouldn't have come as an epiphany, but it most certainly did. It came during a particular session when she suggested we try doing a visual exercise. I trusted her by this point, so I agreed. There, in her counseling office, she placed an empty chair facing me. It was directly across from where I was sitting. It was small. Child sized. At least in my memory it was. She clicked on the side table lamp then flipped off the overhead fluorescent lights. The room became dim. Darkened, yet peaceful. I took a deep breath.

Her shadowy figure spoke. "I'd like you to close your eyes."

I obliged.

After a moment or two, her instruction came again, "Now, slowly open your eyes. Do you see this empty little chair? Are you looking at it?"

I nodded without reply, while my thoughts sassed, *Of course, I see it! You just put it there a moment ago. Shhhhh!* I quieted and cleared my thoughts so that I could hear her next silly command.

She continued, "Okay. Good. Now, I would like you to imagine your child self at four years old. I want you to imagine that four-year-old is now sitting right here in this chair across from you... She's facing you now. Do you see her?"

I fidgeted in my seat.

"Teri? Do you see her?" she gently attempted to confirm.

Once again, my mental banter refused to be muzzled, *What a stupid exercise! I feel ridiculous. I'm glad no one else is here to see this. How embarrassing. I'm not going to do it!* Inside I balked. I belittled. I blatantly refused. The thoughts squirmed, finally making their way out, "No. I don't see her!"

I must admit, even I found my curt response startling. I had no idea why I was pushing back so hard. All I knew for certain was, there was no way I was going to try to imagine myself as a little girl in a little chair for this twisted exercise. What was she trying to prove with all this?

Undaunted by my rudeness, she carefully pressed forward, asking a second time, "Can you visualize her now? Do you see yourself as a child sitting there in front of you? What look is on her face? How do you feel about her?"

"Stop!" I argued. "This is so silly! I don't see her, and I don't want to continue this exercise." By this point my voice was almost pleading.

"Why?" She asked and continued, "Is it that you *can't* or is it that you *don't want to* see her? Why don't you want to see her sitting in that chair?" The counselor relentlessly prompted, by slightly rephrasing her question.

With that final push, the shocking truth came tumbling out of me. "Because I don't like her or anything about her!!!" With that, my voice broke, and tears blurred my eyes.

There it was. In a moment, her chiseling had finally given way. The wall around my childhood, my very identity, cracked open and began crumbling around me. I couldn't seem to stop it. I wanted to snatch the words from the air and put them back where they came from. But it was too late. Out of my own mouth I had spoken it. And now, there was no way to argue with the ugly truth: Clearly, I didn't like Teri. More specifically, I despised the child Teri Hodge.

We both sat there in the silence of this epiphany. My mind was still reeling. What had I just said? I couldn't believe what had just happened. I wasn't ready for this and I didn't understand any of it. I tried to regain my previously stoic composure, thinking somehow, I could play it all down. Quickly, pushing the tears away, I attempted to do damage control starting by giving myself an internal scolding for making such a stupid comment. *Honestly, Teri! Why would you say that? Who doesn't like a four-year-old? Especially when it's your own self!*

Surely, I didn't *hate* myself. That would be so very counterproductive, and heaven knows I saw myself as a very productive person! But here I was, staring at a blatant truth I could not deny. There would be no putting this Jack back into the box. An ill-fitting surprise I didn't want nor asked for was now demanding my attention. The craziest thing was, it had been there, sleeping in me all along. The nauseating thought of facing myself in this unfamiliar way terrified me to the core. But I knew enough to know that true healing couldn't come without the knowledge of what was broken. I just didn't know how, exactly, that healing would happen…

In the darkness of that counseling session, the light had come and wrapped itself around what was broken in me.

God was there… He met me in the chair of a child.

# MY STORY

*Slowing Down to Pray & Reflect*

As I read Chapter One, I am reminded of my own…

When I think about what I just wrote above, it makes me feel…

The most uncomfortable thing I know I've been avoiding is…

In my life, the person / people I trust the most is / are…

When I think about my own childhood, I would describe it as…

When I think about my childhood, it makes me instantly feel…

Describing how I feel about myself as a little kid, I'd say I was…

Describing myself today, I'd say I am…

The lie I have uncovered about the way I see myself is…

# PRAYERS & MEDITATIONS

## *Chapter 1*

Then children were brought to him that he might lay his hands on them and pray. The disciples rebuked the people, but Jesus said, "Let the little children come to me and do not hinder them, for to such belong the kingdom of heaven." Matthew 19:13-14 (ESV)

Even if my father and mother abandon me, the LORD will hold me close. Psalm 27:10 (NLT)

When I am afraid, I put my trust in you. Psalm 56:3 (ESV)

For the LORD is good; his steadfast love endures forever, and his faithfulness to all generations. Psalm 100:5 (ESV)

He reveals the deep and hidden things, he knows what is in the darkness, and the light dwells with him. Daniel 2:22 (ESV)

He uncovers the deeps out of darkness and brings deep darkness to light. Job 12:22 (ESV)

Be strong and courageous. Do not fear or be in dread of them, for it is the LORD your God who goes with you. He will not leave you or forsake you. Deuteronomy 31:6 (ESV)

My Prayer…

# Chapter 2

# Meeting God Before Time

*H*uddling close together, holding our breath, we shared the same thought, *Does she know where we are?* The most threatening thing for little kids like us was about to happen. At that moment, stomping up the sidewalk was the neighborhood bully. And word on the street was that she was looking for us! One of the kids had tipped us off and now we were taking shelter in my backyard. Hunched down on the other side of our garage's back door, I consoled my young friend, "She'll never find us here." Her trusting brown eyes quickly scanned the blue of mine for reassurance.

Still, shivering with fear, she raised her clenched fists upward, tucking them closely under her tiny chin. Then leaning in close, she whispered, "Why is God doing this to us?" I can still recall how her worrisome question caught me completely off guard.

I turned from spying through the crack in the door to address her innocent fear. Knowing in my heart of hearts that her question was unfounded, I confidently replied, "God isn't punishing us. He's not doing this." I might have been young, but instinctively I knew if someone was choosing to intimidate us, it wasn't God's fault. That was their own doing.

Hearing my words, her demeanor relaxed just a little. "Okay..." she replied, dropping her hands back down to her sides. Though I was certain of what I'd just said, her face gave way to what her heart still carried—a mixture of contemplation and disbelief. Even as a little kid, I found her comment surprising.

Many times, I've thought about that summer afternoon when God was mislabeled and blamed for something *I knew* He didn't do. To this day, what I can't put my finger on, is how was it that this assurance came to be *in me*? What brought this certainty of Him, even at such an incredibly early age? And why did I feel the urgent need to console my sweet friend with what I knew?

Those words that day came naturally, flowing right out of me. I knew that I knew that I knew God was *good* and that He could be trusted. In my childlike faith, the truth that I understood about God was as solid as concrete, a foundational slab embedded deeply into my soul. God was no bully. Nor was he responsible for sending a bully our way that day. Somehow this truth had already come to me. God was not some kind of unfounded punisher, who delighted in watching people squirm under His attack.

As a child my memories always included Him. Like my mom, dad and two older brothers, He was simply always there. He was always a part of me. I couldn't recall the first time we'd met. The knowing of Him was there long before a single memory ever was.

There would be days coming, however, when this pure and childlike image of God would be shaken and challenged. Distortions and lies would come. They'd come slowly, so slowly that I would never see them for what they were. I wouldn't recognize them as such. They'd come slyly, so slyly that I wouldn't even know when or how it was happening. I would believe the lies.

Later, I would hate myself for it.

How did everything change? There wasn't any one person or situation to blame. It was more like a culmination of a hundred little things all gathered under one big black umbrella. It was my spiritual portfolio if you will. And like any good investor, I was diversified! A sizable portion of my confusion came at the hands of those I looked up to most, those I'd invested in. The inconsistency of their actions, opposing much of what they claimed to believe, was very confusing to a young girl.

Deliberate attempts to sway, manipulate or simply adjust my line of thinking to match a particular doctrine or belief was commonplace. My young mind didn't question the distortions. I trusted adults to feed me truth and correct my "errors." I blindly did my best to follow what I was taught by those who claimed to be "educated" on things of the Divine. They were more than happy to tell me where my thoughts were out of alignment. Tinkering on my beliefs with their doctrinal wrenches, they'd make their adjustments under my religious hood. At the time, I couldn't see how the very things they touted as "Godly" had actually made them stiff, cold and anything but.

When genuine questions were asked, the calculated answers came laced with manipulation. It was not at all like the innocent conversation between two young girls in a backyard so many years before. The only interest of these self-acclaimed religious know-it-alls seemed to be in convincing me to see things their way.

The simple and innocent knowing of Him I had as a kid, was slowly being silenced by a warped and altered truth. Over time, unknowingly, I would find myself being introduced to "versions" of God. And whether I understood this or not, each would leave its mark on me, as I drifted from one to the next.

My youngest introduction came when I met Flannel Board God and His mini-me-in-sandals son, Jesus. We were properly introduced in my childhood Sunday school class. These flannel cutouts, along with all their sidekicks, Moses, Noah and the whole disciple gang, were one-dimensionally flat, faded and frayed. Over and over, God and his friends would lose their flannel grip, fluttering from the board only to be rescued from the freckled-white laminate floor of the classroom. This God was lukewarm milk and stale cookies. The

Flannel Board Posse was as boring and out of date as my teacher's beehive hairdo. I just wanted the playground.

As I got a little older, I began to read. This is when I met Storybook God. He was the one who did all those Old Testament miracles, like parting the Red Sea and rescuing Noah's family along with all those animals from a gigantic flood. Some of these stories seemed familiar from my earlier days with Flannel Board God, but now, reading them on my own was so much better! The words were easy to follow and the images vibrantly detailed. The only problem was, Storybook God could only be found there on the pages. Though I'd loved and memorized many of these stories as a kid, they held no context for me. In this girl's life, I had no need for an ark, nor to have a sea parted on my behalf. The bookshelf remained the place I'd go to find Storybook God.

Later, in my young teen years, I met Personal Janitor God. Thank goodness for Him. Personal Janitor God was awesome, a favorite for sure! I met Him while sitting in the pew on Sunday hearing about my sins. I was promised that Personal Janitor God would always show up and make things better. He'd wash what I'd stained and make it brand new. Even better, He could transform my darkest mistakes into snowy white innocence. With a broom, a mop, and a bucket of water, whatever I needed, He'd be beckon-call ready to jump in and clean up each time I'd make a mess of things. No problem was too big or too small for Janitor God to handle! All I had to do was simply ask and it would be done in a blink. No need for accountability or learning curves. It will be as if it never happened! Being quite prone to creating messes, I called on Him a lot.

Santa Claus God dropped in somewhere in the middle of those years. I'd heard several rumors about Him. They sounded pretty good to me. In a nutshell, I was told if I behave nicely, I'd make the good list. He'd even reward me with gifts! But there was this catch. Just being good was never quite good enough. I must also BELIEVE and never doubt! It was a combo deal. It was a rare occurrence when I felt I made the good list long enough to ask for something *really* special. If I did manage a streak of good behavior, it was certain I deserved something special. But, having pride in myself for being so good would inadvertently knock me back off the list. Santa Claus God kept a keen eye on not only my behaviors but my thoughts and emotions too. Nothing slid by Him. He was always keeping track!

When I found myself in a tight spot, I learned about Negotiator God. With Him, it's all about the barter. There's always a trade going on—so you'd want to get in on the deal. What did you have to offer? What were you willing to trade? If you gave up this, He might give you that. If you would do this for Him, He may do that for you. It was strictly even Steven. A contractual agreement between me and Negotiator God was promised to be ironclad. I'd cross my heart and promise to keep up my end of the bargain—after all a deal was a deal. Those contracts usually ended with a default on my end. But even if I hurriedly did my part, still, that was no grounds to assume He would do likewise. The rules of the contract were clearly stated upfront: I was to promptly fulfill my part and He could take as long as He wanted to fulfill His end. My job was to make sure I kept the faith and remained patient. Anything less was unacceptable. Many times, I'd grow tired in the waiting and simply give up the whole thing. Each time this happened, I'd walk away a little more bitter.

By my late teens I was often threatened by Hell, Fire and Brimstone God. Being introduced to Him through a screaming red-faced pastor, the image is forever burned into my brain. The Hell, Fire and Brimstone God was straight-up terrifying. He scared the bajeebies out of me. There was no love, there was only anger. And there was nothing anyone could do or say to cool that anger. He was insatiable, unpleasable, so there was no point in trying. By the time we'd met, I was informed He'd already punched my one-way ticket to Hell. In fact, I was on my way there already. The message was hopelessly clear. I'd better hurry and start that begging. Maybe, just maybe, if I pleaded for mercy long enough, He'd yank me from those flames at the very last second. But not before He got the chance to make me suffer a little more. After all I'd put Him through, I deserved nothing less. I was told how He HATED the things I'd done but it was conveyed to me more like this: He hated ME for the things I'd done. He saw me as the ultimate loser so disappointingly far from His heavenly ideal. He regretted creating me. I'd never measure up and that made Him furious. I had more than my share of nightmares thanks to Him.

Punisher God was a spinoff of Hell, Fire and Brimstone God. He was the one dishing out the painful consequences for my continual screw ups and bad decisions. I was always in trouble with Him, and payment was constantly due. Punisher God delighted in punishment. Punishing people was the whole reason He existed. He was constantly creating new ways to make sure I paid dearly for my sins. The bigger the error, the harsher the punishment. I was not to be fooled. No matter how smooth life might seem to be going, it would only be only a matter of time before His wrath would be catching up with me. I was assured that my sin-bill was so monstrous, I could never really pay the debt off completely. It was like a revolving account on which I was constantly charging. Punishment was the only currency He accepted for payment. There was no way out of it. There's no avoiding Punisher God. You'd better watch every step!

With all these God versions crossing my path, I would continue to search. This couldn't be the end. I knew something was missing. The innocent connection with the God from my childhood, was now marred and no longer reliable. I had lost that preciously simple clarity little by little at the hand of each of them. And now, as an adult, I strove to grasp that innocent peace once more. Eventually, all of this drove me straight under the rule of Perfectionist God, the kingpin of religion. Perfectionist God was basically all the others rolled into one. But this God was far more clever, much more sly in His delivery. Perfectionist God might have been a collaboration, but He offered me something more enticing than any of the others ever could. Perfectionist God offered me CONTROL.

I liked the idea of this God right away. He was someone I could work with. He was happy to give me that bullet point list and to let me know exactly what was expected of me. This worked so well for me. After all, I loved bullet point lists. There was no guesswork. With Perfectionist God, there was no mystery where I stood with Him. It was all laid out in black and white, all of it, right there in the Bible! To please Him and to avoid His guilt, all I would have to do is get it right the first time. If I had a question, I could simply look up the answer in His rule book. If I got confused, I simply made an appointment for clarification from those who knew more than me. I could go straight to the ones who ran the place. They'd interpret what He wanted from me. It could get confusing with so many rules to obey. Some were golden and some were written on stone tablets, but all were to be followed to the very last letter. There were no exceptions. I found Him to be a nice God when I had a lengthy stretch of obedience. It was when I failed that we had problems. Big problems. When I'd blow it, I knew Perfectionist God would soon be consulting with all the other gods to decide my fate. There was a small chance He'd toss me a scrap of mercy, but it was best not to take any chances. The three strikes rule was always out there looming. Better to throw myself on the mercy of the court as a repeat offender.

Being raised in a legalistic setting, there were times I thought I must've been on the fast track with Perfectionist God. I constantly did my best to stay on His good side. There were brownie points to earn, and I was all about those brownie points! I gladly put in the hours. Being well-acquainted with His to-do list, I memorized most of His rules. All of this offered me a sweet sense of "godly" purpose. The arrogant self-appointed validation was a sheer bonus. With all my hard work, I thought I'd arrived. After giving Him all my time, surely I'd become one of His favorites. I loved the perks of being Perfectionist God's "good girl." Knowing upfront what was required of me gave me that sense of control I craved. In my little dysfunctional world, I longed for security with no surprises. Perfectionism came with the promise that I could make that happen. Not surprisingly, I'd become addicted to performance. Like a junkie looking for the next fix, perfectionism gave me a way to tap into an immediate, yet false, comfort. I knew how to jump through hoops for acceptance. I knew how to perform for love. It came so naturally. I'd been training in it all my life.

I was blind to the reality of what was actually happening and what I couldn't see was killing me. My attempts to live life within such a tight margin was ludicrous. It was impossible. Yet I kept at it, with no room for error. In my endless trying (and failing), it would be just a matter of time before it took its relentless toll.

Like juggling fine china, one small slip of the hand and everything would come crashing down. Even the best attempts would eventually end up shattering into pieces. Since the responsibility rested solely on me, so did the cleanup. I accepted that. Each time, I'd frantically sweep up the fragments of my failures and try to put my life back into place. But it wouldn't be long before it would happen again. Then again. The words of the red-faced pastor would echo their scoldings. I'd hear the overwhelming chides reminding me that *breaking one rule was the same as breaking them all!* Like a fish swimming circles in his bowl, my inability to go a day without some blunder would cause me to frantically strive all the harder.

The more I tried, the sadder I became.

It was incredibly ironic, I had been so busy checking the behavioral boxes, that I never saw the blaring truth right in front of me. Spending my life chasing the illusion of perfection was robbing me of the life I was truly meant to live.

These relentless God beliefs had driven me to the very edge of myself and left me there, with nothing. I was like a soldier with the phantom pain of a missing leg lost in battle. There was such an incessant need to hit this elusive mark, despite being surrounded on every side by spiritual and emotional carnage.

The damage was everywhere. My seven-year marriage had slid over a cliff to its final demise. My two little girls were hurting at having their home torn apart. Relatives and longtime friends had slowly begun making themselves scarce. I hadn't looked up long enough to see how incredibly alone I'd become. I was a disgrace. Eventually, the idea of attending church became a literal joke. A mockery— reminding me of the perfect little life that I would never have. I couldn't muster the faintest prayer. It seemed too far away from where I now stood. And I was tired. What once had been my beacon of hope had now become the very last place I wanted to go.

Despite my fighting to ignore it, reality was pushing itself in on me. It was more than I could handle. It seemed everything I'd touched, somehow, I'd ruined. No matter how hard I'd tried, I couldn't seem to help but mess life up somehow. If perfection were obtainable, clearly I would never get there. Now facing the jumbled wreckage of my multiple failings, I knew that my days with Him were numbered. Following His rules perfectly had proved to be a ruse, a bait and switch. An unobtainable, impossible task. The bar had always been set way too high.

My bones ached with an utter disgust in myself. Surely this God, who focuses on my perfection, had given up on me as well. I imagined His stance, arms folded rigidly with His back turned coldly toward me. It was over. My mistakes had piled so high by this point, there was no way to get around them. How very disappointing I'd been to Him. My giant list of wrongs now buried me. The never-ending repentance prayers seemed to remain unheard. I was suffocating under the load of regrets. There would be no way out.

These thoughts soon turned into haunting questions. What's *the point of going on like this? All I've ever done is mess up my life and the lives of those I love most. I've even alienated God! I have no one to blame but myself. Surely everyone would be better off without me?*

I'd hit rock bottom. I could find no hope to move forward nor any strength to go back to what was.

With nothing left to lose, I decided to take a chance on letting my mom in on my inner torture which was nearing its final crescendo.

It was late in the afternoon on an average day. We were heading back from running errands. Mom, who was completely unaware of what I was contemplating, had simply called earlier that day to ask if I would keep her company for a few hours while she knocked out her list of errands. I'd obliged hoping to get my mind off the impending doom. Just getting out of the house would provide some relief.

Our time together was pleasantly uneventful until we headed for home. Riding shotgun while she drove, I reasoned, if I was going to mention my plight, it would need to be now. She was just about to crest the final hill toward her house. Slightly pivoting in my seat, I turned my whole body in her direction. Then I dropped the bomb into her lap.

"Hey Mom? Is it normal to think about dying?" the shocking words came without warning. They also came without emotion, as if I were asking her to pass me the ketchup.

Like an ice cube stuck in the air, time froze the moment I said it. I'd hit her with a full 220 volts and even from her side view, I could see the shock as it ripped across her entire face. Immediately, she turned, locking eyes with me for just a moment. It felt like an eternity. Then, as if in slow motion, she turned back to the road in front of her before saying a word.

"What do you mean, Teri? Do you think about dying?" she asked gently. She kept her gaze straight ahead while latently attempting to mask over her already exposed concern.

I nodded slightly while giving a robotic reply, "Yes. Do you think that's normal?"

"Well…," she hesitated to fully answer, choosing her next words carefully. "How often do you think about it?"

"Oh... Every day." I flatly confessed with a slight shrug.

She then sighed the heaviest sigh I've ever heard. "No, Teri. That's not normal." Her troubled voice softened as it trickled off to silence.

I watched her eyebrows furrow, though her eyes remained staring straight ahead. Pulling into the driveway, there was nothing left to say.

God had surely left me—or so I believed.

I was 26.

# MY STORY

*Slowing Down to Pray & Reflect*

As I read Chapter Two, I was reminded of my own…

When I think about what I just wrote, it makes me feel…

My description of God…

My beliefs about God come from…

How I feel about God right now…

How I think God feels about me right now…

The lie I have uncovered about God is…

# PRAYERS & MEDITATIONS

## *Chapter 2*

Before I formed you in the womb I knew you, and before you were born I consecrated you.  Jeremiah 1:5 (ESV)

For you formed my inward parts; you knitted me together in my mother's womb. I praise you, for I am fearfully and wonderfully made. Wonderful are your works; my soul knows it very well. Psalm 139:13-14 (ESV)

My frame was not hidden from you, when I was being made in secret, intricately woven in the depths of the earth. Your eyes saw my unformed substance; in your book were written, every one of them, the days that were formed for me, when as yet there was none of them. Psalm 139:15-16 (ESV)

The LORD is near to the brokenhearted and saves the crushed in spirit.  Psalm 34:18 (ESV)

Therefore, confess your sins one to another and pray for one another, that you may be healed. The prayer of a righteous man has great power as it is working.  James 5:16 (ESV)

Are you tired? Worn out? Burned out on religion? Come to me. Get away with me and you'll recover your life. I'll show you how to take a real rest. Matthew 11:28 (MSG)

A hurricane wind ripped through the mountains and shattered the rocks before GOD, but GOD wasn't to be found in the wind; after the wind an earthquake, but GOD wasn't in the earthquake; and after the earthquake fire, but God wasn't in the fire; and after the fire a gentle and quiet whisper. 1 Kings 19:11-12 (MSG)

My Prayer…

# Chapter 3

# MEETING GOD
# IN MY SHAME

*In* the corner of our kitchen where two cabinets came together, I collapsed into a hopeless pile on the cold linoleum floor. Not bothering to flip on the light before dropping to the ground, I preferred not to see anything anyway. Alone, I sat rocking back and forth in the strange comfort of the blackness. Hugging my knees to my chest, I couldn't stop the crying. It was 2:00 am and the realization of everything happening in my life had again woken me from another night's sleep.

It seemed these times in the kitchen had become a self-soothing routine. Being a single mom of two young ones, during the day I had to keep it together. This seemed the only time I could let it go and apparently my internal clock knew it. The darkness of depression had steadily grown thick. I couldn't escape it by sleeping and my days were spent trying to hide it. Despite the distractions of a graveyard shift and daytime with the kids, at any given moment I could find myself sucked back into that black hole. The nights haunted and the mornings brought heaviness—my failures repeatedly hitting me before the sun filled the room.

I felt the constant jabs of guilt when I thought of my beautiful girls, so young and innocent. They didn't ask for any of this. Each time I'd look into their huge blue eyes I was reminded of all they'd lost. I was changing the course of their lives forever and that couldn't be undone. It was heartbreaking. They deserved so much better, and I felt such shame that I couldn't deliver the best for them. I loved them more than life itself and I had failed them unforgivably. What kind of mom can't find a way to keep her family together? Waves of regret endlessly rolled in, whispering my worthlessness back to me.

This failed marriage proved the worst of my fears. I would never be enough. I could never make this right. The day I signed the divorce papers felt like the day I signed away my faith. It was a death sentence to my perfection-driven goals that hoped to please a Perfectionist God. I would now never be GRADE A acceptable in His eyes, nor my own eyes. And certainly, never again in the eyes of the church. All I could see from that point forward was the mess I'd made of my life and the failure I'd become. How could I go on?

Other than the confession to my mom driving in the car that day, no one knew how dangerously close to the edge I'd been walking. I'm not sure there were many that cared at the time. I'd alienated quite a few people along the way. God and I weren't speaking. I was sure He'd left the building. It wasn't good. We'd reached an impossible impasse. I knew He had His standards, and I knew I couldn't meet them. I felt I'd worn out every inch of His patience and now He was over it. When I looked around me, the facts were everywhere, blatantly staring me in the face. I was exhausted from being in constant spiritual survival mode. I was trying to hang on to God, but my mind and my body had grown weak, aching for rest that never came.

It felt like chewing a limb off, but there seemed no options left. The way I saw it, there were only two ways to make the madness stop. The first option would escalate my eternal fate much faster than the second. The second, seemed the only choice that would leave me still breathing. If I could just find a way to get a little more time, I could fix things somehow. I could fix myself. I could fix my relationships with others. I could fix my relationship with God. I just needed time. I could no longer think straight. I had no strength left. If I took a break, I reasoned, maybe I could put all of this on pause and simply rest. It was worth a try. This seemed like the only way I could manage staying on the planet for another day.

So, I did the unthinkable. I had a break-up talk with God. I told Him I couldn't live this way anymore. I needed some space. I needed time to clear my head.

I told Him it was me to blame, never Him. I admitted the failures were a hundred percent on me, my fault, alone. I tried to explain how very exhausted I'd become. I needed some time to rest. A short break was all I was asking for. Maybe then, I could come back stronger, finally able to give Him what He wanted from me. I let him know that even though we'd had distance between us for a while now, I wasn't throwing our relationship away, I was simply placing Him on a shelf for a little while. I assured Him that soon I would be back, that is if He would still have me. I wasn't saying *goodbye*. It was just: *see you later.* And with that, it was done. This time, I didn't wait for His reply.

Soon, I found the rest I so desperately needed was not going to come that easily. Instead, no matter how I tried to numb it, guilt continued to gnaw at my insides as months went by. I dragged the shame with me, everywhere I went. The cloud of my failures continually hung over my shoulder reminding me I would never deserve forgiveness. I would never get a re-do.

The added bonus came in the profound loneliness that followed. Many times, I wondered how I would be able to get out of bed to face all that lay ahead. But soon, a tousle-headed little girl would call, "Mommy" from the other room. Their tiny voices would remind me of why I was still here. They continued to pull me into another day.

I met David in the middle of this dark season. Since I was running from God at the time, he, being agnostic, seemed like the safest place to land. Being easy to talk to and holding no judgments of me, it was an easy friendship from the start. I was clear with him upfront, that friendship was all I was offering.

Though at the beginning he didn't believe in God the way I did, he seemed to understand and respect where I was coming from. I explained how making vows to God is a very big deal and I'd broken mine getting divorced. I told him the way I saw things, I quite possibly might never be "allowed" to marry again and certainly not to someone who didn't share a faith in God. None of these confessions seemed to detour him. They only made him more inquisitive about this mysterious God that I had put on hold.

One evening, we were sitting together talking, when he openly began sharing the reasons for his disbelief. As he told his story, I could piece it together, seeing from his eyes why he had come to the conclusions he had made. It made sense to me. I was not at all surprised that his life situations had led him to a deliberate absence of faith. I felt no compulsion to correct him. No desire to smugly point out doctrine, as had happened to me so many times before. No. This was sacred between us. He trusted me with this, his story. It was real, tangible and honest. It deserved to be recognized, not arrogantly dismissed. What did surprise me, however, was when he got to the part where he asked me, "So what do I have to give up to become a Christian?" He knocked me over with that one. I certainly didn't see that coming!

Here's when things got interesting. I was in the middle of a faith crisis, remember? I couldn't find my way through the blunders created by my own two hands let alone lead anybody else anywhere. The last person he should be asking was the colossal failure that had to take a break from God. Yet, there in that moment, none of that came out of my mouth. None of that religiosity even entered my mind.

What did come was as simple as what came to me long ago, as a little girl. It was the same uncomplicated Spirit, the one that was with me years ago in my backyard with my preschool friend. This Spirit was still there, giving me words of hope to share with Dave. "You don't have to give anything up. It's not like that. That would be trying to be a Christian from the outside in. That way never works. You simply accept Him. Accept that He wants to help you. Allow Him room in your heart. That's it. When you authentically do that, you'll find yourself slowly changing from the inside out." Wow! All of this coming from the woman who relentlessly struggled with perfectionism. But, as I said these words to him, I knew deep inside, what I was telling him was the truth. David could have this relationship with God. It was right there if he wanted it. Then just as quickly as these hopeful words left my lips, my own failings sprang up and shoved them back down my throat. The familiar condemning thoughts were quick to remind me that even though what I just shared was true for Dave, it was not true for me. I was a major screw up. My faith ship had sailed. It was so weird to me how I could so easily share this hope with Dave, while I sat smudged and dirtied in my own shipwrecked faith. How could both of these truths coexist inside me—one for him and another for me? Thank goodness he didn't notice the crazy tug of war going on inside my head. He was pondering what he'd just heard. Something Divine was happening in that moment for him. It was the beginning of something incredible that would change his life forever.

Regarding the relationship between David and I, there was no "biblical reason" I could expect anything more than what we presently shared as close friends. I felt God was being more than generous giving me this much. After all, I was divorced. How could God ever forgive that? I did what I could to remember my second-class state and chose to simply be grateful for what I'd been given.

It was a fine and good plan to say we would remain just friends, but over time the friend-feelings between us eventually grew into more. Each time I would sense this happening, I would immediately cool things down. I'd put space between us as needed to keep things light. If that didn't work, I'd abruptly stop seeing him all together. I had a life to fix. Not to complicate. I needed to keep my head and my path clear. There was no way that this relationship could go any further than what it was. When it came to anything more than that, I was fairly convinced that there was no way it could be part of a Divine plan. The rules I learned said God doesn't allow remarriage—ever! Still, despite my best efforts, it would only be a week or two until I missed my friend so much that I'd end up calling him. We'd promise to reset the friend meter and begin hanging out again. But each time, the feelings would pick right back up where they'd left off. Because of this, it wouldn't be long until I'd end things again. And again. And again. I drove us both nuts.

No matter how many times I'd push him away, David would patiently wait for me to return. There was something else going on among all the comings and goings in our relationship. David's faith was growing more curious, slowly stronger with each passing day. It wasn't long before finally, he decided to give his life to Christ. David became a Christian.

It was kind of ironic. David had found his hope and his own faith, while sitting with me smack in the middle of my faith crisis. I found it incredible how it all started with that simple question he posed that day. Then how the words of encouragement came immediately to answer, through me of all people. The one who struggled with "doing it right." How interesting that God would use this to remind me that despite all my troubles and doubts, He had never left me. Even if I had tried to leave Him.

Who was I fooling? I couldn't run from this God. I couldn't hide. I couldn't even take a little break to catch my breath. Even when I didn't understand, He wasn't leaving me alone to figure it out.

Though the pulse of my relationship with God had grown faint, it was still there, still beating. I missed Him. I wanted to come home. It was time. I wanted this breakup with God to be over.

Still, even though He proved to me He hadn't left me, I still feared that when it came right down to it, maybe He wouldn't take me back. I know that sounds silly. But it was a real and lingering fear. What would I do if God didn't want to take me back? What was He going to say when He saw me coming? And that I wasn't coming back alone? David, now a believer, had become woven into my story. I had to be honest about that. I couldn't deny the love that had grown between us. Together we agreed to hand Him all of this, all of us. We would let go and trust the outcome to His capable hands.

Whatever way He would receive me, I was willing to accept. Whatever the outcome, whatever He wanted in all of this, I knew that I knew one thing for certain: the tiny whisper that still told me, God is good. It was going to be okay—no matter what happened next.

So, despite the shame of my dirty scrapes and bruises, I headed back toward Him. I came as I was, without trying to clean up first. This was new for me, and I had no idea what it looked like. This time, I was not returning to a building. I was not returning to a clergy or to anyone who touted all the "right" answers. My sights were set on Him alone. No one else would do. I knew I needed God Himself.

For the first time in a long time, I began to pray.

God had met me in the middle of my shame.

# MY STORY

*Slowing Down to Pray & Reflect*

As I read Chapter Three, I was reminded of my own…

When I think about what I just wrote, it makes me feel…

The thing that keeps me up at night is…

What troubles me the most about this is…

I struggle to feel forgiven for…

Praying about this seems…

Where I feel God might be right now…

The lie I have uncovered about my shame is…

# PRAYERS & MEDITATIONS

*Chapter 3*

So, he told them this parable: "What man of you, having a hundred sheep, if he has lost one of them, does not leave the ninety-nine in the open country, and go after the one that is lost, until he finds it? And when it is found, he lays it on his shoulders, rejoicing." Luke 15:3-6 (ESV)

Where shall I go from your Spirit? Or where shall I flee from your presence? If I ascend to heaven, you are there. If I make my bed in Sheol, you are there! If I take the wings of the morning and dwell in the uttermost parts of the sea, even then your hand shall lead me and your right hand shall hold me. Psalm 139:7-10 (ESV)

If I say, "Surely the darkness shall cover me, and the light about me be night," even then darkness is not dark to you; the night is bright as the day, for the darkness is as light with you. Psalm 139:11-12 (ESV)

And rend your hearts and not your garments. Return to the LORD your God, for he is gracious and merciful, slow to anger, and abounding in steadfast love; and he relents over disaster. Joel 2:13 (ESV)

I will rise and go to my father, and I will say to him, "Father, I have sinned against heaven and before you. I am no longer worthy to be called your son. Treat me as one of your hired servants." But while he was still a long way off, his father saw him and felt compassion, and ran and embraced him and kissed him." Luke 15:18-20. (ESV)

My Prayer…

# Chapter 4

# Meeting
# God at Sunset

early two years had gone by since David and I had first met. During that time, he'd been there for me, supportively helping me again and again. He grew to be my closest companion, my confidant, and my best friend.

He'd proven his strong commitment to all of us, to me as well as to my two girls. We were now spending much of our free time together. From nightly meals around the dinner table, to weekend outings, he seemed to bring the missing piece to our little clan. He had a lot to do with bringing fun and laughter once again into the house. There was silliness too.

He was there for many of the kids' firsts. Some of those firsts came directly because of him. He'd bought the girls their first roller skates, happily spending hours teaching them how to balance. He grinned with pride when they'd finally wabbled along on their own, their bright pink wheels rolling down the front walkway. He was the one who taught them how to ride a bike and how to swim. Many hours were filled with giggles when he'd agree to a game of Pretty Princess. He'd sit willingly in the middle of the family room floor while they adorned him with plastic clip-on earrings, beaded necklaces, and a coveted golden plastic jeweled crown. Hair scrunchies were an optional part of the glam. David was there, being a great sport. Not only was he good to me, but he also genuinely adored my girls. He loved making them happy. And nothing pleased my mama heart more.

The roots of our relationship grew deeper with each experience shared together, solidifying this bond between us. It was useless to ignore the probability that an eventual proposal would be coming in the not-too-distant future. You'd think this hint would've made me happy, but the thought of it caused an uneasiness in me. Though life was falling into place, still, a faint nagging remained in the back of my mind. My relationship with God was still a long way from where I'd wanted it to be. And now in the current situation, I had more doubts than ever about how God saw me. Perfectionism or no perfectionism, I knew what the Bible said. Those scriptural waters still ran deep in me. They hadn't changed. I never was quite ready to face what I'd been taught—*If I remarry, it's a permanent sin against God. In this case, I will NEVER be forgiven.* I believed every word of the Bible to be God breathed. Believing this wasn't the same thing as being legalistic or religious. The Bible held the truth and I wanted to honor the truth. But the people in charge of that truth had preached something different in my ear. I was having a tough time untangling the truth from the lie.

For a while now I'd been asking God for guidance on the direction I was to go with David. I watched and waited for some kind of sign to tell me what to do. So far, nothing was on the horizon. Could it be there would be no sign because the writing was already on the wall? Probably. I had to admit to myself that it was highly unlikely that His Divine Plan for my life included a permanent future with David. Maybe we would be able to keep a token friendship, but I still had a hard time believing He would ever allow me a second "I Do."

If I knew this relationship between us was doomed by the Almighty, why the hesitation to end it? The reason was crystal clear to me, I didn't want anyone to hurt. I wanted to avoid *their* pain. My children had already seen more than their fair share of it. David certainly didn't deserve heartbreak; he'd been nothing but kind to me. To all of us. As far as my own heart, I was willing to accept the pain of a break up as deserved retribution. I could deal with that. But what if I was wrong? I would negatively impact all four of our futures for no reason at all. I just couldn't pull the trigger yet because I simply wasn't sure what to do.

What I did know was that I genuinely wanted to follow God doing whatever He commanded. It became all that mattered to me. Whether we stayed together or ended things, I knew if I followed Him, though I might not understand it at the time, ultimately it would be for everyone's good. I knew God was the one who stirred Dave's heart towards Him to begin with. But losing me and the girls might risk shaking that newfound faith, wouldn't it? I could see the enormous impact this decision would create. It was much too important to wing it, simply going by my feelings. I had to wait on God. My heart wanted to do the right thing, but I was so unsure which way to go. I believed if I allowed God to lead, He'd cause something to happen that would force me into the right direction.

I'd been asking for that direction for a while now. It had been nearly two years of waiting and it felt like time was running out.

One night, I woke from a dead sleep with a strange prompting. I felt an urgency to get up and read my Bible, right then. It was such a strong pull that I instantly obeyed it. Groggily, I slipped out of bed and felt my way down the dark hallway to the living room. I slowly seated myself on the couch, leaning over to click on the lamp next to me. My Bible was right there on the coffee table. Reverently I lifted it, setting it gently on my lap. It was the middle of the night! What was happening? Had God decided this would be a good time to talk to me? If He had, I wanted to hear every word. Taking the moment seriously, I began to pray: *You've woken me up and clearly have my attention now. Show me what you want me to see, Lord. Please tell me what you want me to do.* Gently, I opened my Bible, dropping my eyes and focusing on the verse written there in front of me. Surely this would be my answer! The quietness of the night added to the sacredness of the moment. I would take in every word. I began to read. *"When you fast, do not look somber as the hypocrites do, for they disfigure their faces to show others they are fasting…"* FASTING? I was extremely disappointed with the text. I was looking for His guidance on remarriage not how to perform some Old Testament ritual! None of this made sense to me. Closing the Bible, I set it back on the table and turned off the light. Slipping back into bed, I chalked the whole thing up to the pizza I'd eaten the night before.

Until it happened again the next night.

Once again, I woke out of a dead sleep and immediately felt compelled to get up and read my Bible. *This is crazy!* I thought to myself as I slid my feet into my slippers. Again, out to the living room I went, clicking on the light for a second night in a row. Again, I placed my Bible onto my lap. Praying even harder this time, *Dear Lord, please show me. What do you want from me? I'll do whatever you ask, just please show me what you want me to know*! With that I opened His word. I noticed that I'd opened it to a different place in the Bible than I had the night before. But there in front of me, I could not believe my eyes: Another scripture, a different scripture on fasting! *Are you kidding me?* I questioned the Almighty. Whatever this was, the message was lost on me. I wasn't getting the connection. What did fasting have to do with the guilt of a failed marriage and the fate of my future with or without David? How did this have anything to do with my situation? Now with a mixture of confusion and frustration, I closed the Bible and again headed back to bed. We had a big weekend coming up and it was starting this morning—in just a few hours. I couldn't afford to lose any more sleep trying to decipher this heavenly code.

Despite my interruption of sleep, we left on time that morning with girls in tow. We were headed toward the coast to a family reunion on Dave's side. The kids loved the beach and all of us were excited to attend. The idea of a weekend away watching them play and meeting family sounded just like what we needed. Once we arrived and unloaded the truck, Dave quickly set up our little tent and campsite. I rolled out four sleeping bags, lining them side by side under the pointy canvas. Everything was set.

After smores and campfire stories with everyone, we headed back to our little tent for a night's sleep under the stars. Barely able to slide into their bags, the girls were out for the count in minutes. In this sweet setting, a grateful calmness lulled me to sleep as well. That is until about halfway through the night.

For the third night in a row, as if right on que, I awoke. The heavenly call came. *"Get up and read."* But this time I was sausaged between three other people staring at a canvas ceiling! I couldn't simply get up and click on a light. I was in a sleeping bag for heaven's sake! What the heck was going on? I let God in on my frustration, *I want to get up and grab my Bible, I really do. But clearly that can't happen tonight. You know I want Your will for my life, but if you're going to wake me up like this, you're just going to have to say it. You're gonna have to tell me what it is you're trying to show me! Because I'm not getting out of this sleeping bag and I'm certainly NOT going out there in the dark!*

Immediately, a VERY clear word interrupted me. *"Fast!"* Instantly, the two scriptures that I'd previously read the last two nights flashed across my mind. I connected the dots even though it made no sense. *Each time you got up and read, it was about fasting...*

With the thought so clearly present, I ventured to ask, *Is that you God? Are you telling me to fast?*

Then in the next moment He spoke again. His words shot like lightning straight down into my soul. They froze me in place, there was no denying the clarity. *"If you want your answer, then fast!"*

*Wow. Did that just happen? Did God just speak to me right here in my tiny little tent?* Incredible… and crazy. I had to be sure.

I remember vividly what I said to Him next: *God, if this really is you, then yes, I will fast tomorrow. I don't understand it, I don't know why you're asking me to do this, but okay. I will do it. And just so I'll know that this is really you, and not my own imagination, please don't let anyone notice when I'm not eating tomorrow. If no one says a word, I'll know this is really You. It will be strictly between You and me. Please don't make your sign something vague, like a dream or something obscure where I'm left to decipher it. God, you know I need something OBVIOUS, like a brick in the head! I don't want to be left wondering if I've missed it, so if it's okay, I would like my sign by tomorrow's sunset.*

Yes, this is exactly what I said. And no, I don't encourage people to dictate orders to God or give Him time limits. I can't explain why I did it but, in that moment, it just came out that way. Then as quickly as the moment came, it ended, leaving a peace behind. That peace settled my bones as it filled the night air around me, as if He were saying, *"I've heard you."* With that I fell asleep for the rest of the night.

The next morning, I woke, bright with anticipation, knowing this would be the day my life would take its destined direction. I'd finally get the clarity I'd been praying for so long. I could hardly wait! I dressed the kids then, bending forward on one knee, I tugged upward on the tent's zipper. Awkwardly angling one foot out of the flap, then the other, I tried not to trip. Both girls followed, stepping through the pint-sized flapping mesh door. David was already outside, sipping his coffee through the steam it created.

Before I could even say good morning, Dave's mom appeared out of nowhere, handing me a paper plate of her freshly made breakfast. *Okay, here we go!* I thought to myself. How would I manage to get out of eating what had just been thoughtfully given to me? I didn't want to hurt her feelings. This would be tricky. I reminded God how I'd asked Him to make it where no one noticed when I wasn't eating. If his mom didn't notice that I wasn't eating the breakfast she'd just prepared, I'd be amazed. Taking the plate from her hands I turned and immediately set it down in front of my daughter who was now scooting up to the table. Sliding an empty Styrofoam cup from the top of the stack, I walked over and poured myself some coffee, lingering there a moment or two before coming back to join everyone. Quietly, maneuvering my legs over the bench, I slid in next to David. I sat there with nothing in front of me but a little white cup. Every other person at the table, including my girls, had a plateful of breakfast in front of them. I was the only one not eating. It was blaringly obvious in such close quarters. Mysteriously no one, including David, seemed to notice. Interesting. So far so good… My faith grew just sitting there at the picnic table.

As the day progressed, I witnessed time and time again that not one word came from anyone when I'd passed on the food and treats throughout the day. My heart raced as I thought of my secret fasting agreement with God. Surely these past few nights had been Him speaking to me! This was really happening. I floated through the day in awe. I knew I would finally get my answer. But my excitement slowly began to wane as the day went on, hours passing with no sign in sight. Nothing had come to me yet. It was now reaching into late afternoon. The end of the day was approaching. What could possibly happen with this short amount of daylight left? I fought the familiar sinking feeling of disappointment. Maybe I wanted this so bad, it really was all in my head.

Then it hit me. What if David had a plan to break up with me? Maybe he didn't want to spoil the day so he's waiting until late afternoon? God was going to answer me by a break up with Dave. My heart panged at the thought, but it was the only thing that made sense. I concluded that if it was Dave's idea, then it wouldn't hurt him. And if this is God's plan then He'll take care of the girls as well. *That must be it!* What else could it be? I began praying for strength to endure the impending pain that was coming before the day's end. After all, I had requested this sign before sunset.

Sure enough, when the last of the dinner tables were cleared, David pulled me aside. "Everyone's decided to walk down to the beach to watch the sunset…" he began. Hearing him say the word, *sunset*, felt like a knife through my heart. He had no clue that I already knew what was coming. "Would you mind hanging back here with me for a minute? I'd like to talk to you. Mom's okay with taking the girls ahead with her." *Here it comes, I know it.*

With my heart sinking inches by the moment, I reluctantly agreed and sent the girls with his mom. They joined the rest of the family in an early evening stroll to watch the sun's afternoon dance on the golden waves. This was supposed to be the day of my new beginning. The answer to my prayers. It still was, it just wasn't turning out the way I'd hoped for.

Once everyone had left for the walk, David called me to him. We stood there, alone at the campsite. He took my hands into his. I wasn't looking at him. Instead, I bounced my eyes from one tree to the next, hoping I wouldn't cry. That would only make things worse. Slowly clearing his throat, he began by telling me how he appreciated me coming on this trip, despite having a cold coming on. Knowing that I was willing to join him, when I might have preferred to stay home with a box of tissues, meant a lot to him. He just wanted to say thank you. He then scooped his arm around my waist and pulled me in close. We stood there hugging.

*Wait! Whaaaat???* What was happening? This didn't make sense. With every word he'd just said, I'd braced myself for the coming "but." *Thank you for being here, BUT it's over. I appreciate you, BUT I'm secretly not happy. I care about you BUT we're breaking up.* Where was the big BUT? I pulled away from his chest and searched his smiling face. All the words he'd said had been so kind. They were sweet and caring. Clearly no break up was coming. The big talk he wanted to have with me was nothing more than to share with me how special I was to him, how happy it made him just having me and the girls there with him.

He then ended the moment with the lighthearted invitation, "So… Do you want to go watch the sunset with everyone now?"

I stood there totally confused. He gave me another hug, dismissing my odd behavior as a byproduct of the cold I was getting over. We then headed hand in hand toward the winding beach path that would join us with the rest of the family.

As we walked together, my mind was all over the place. It was clear he had zero intention of breaking up with me. That was now obvious. In fact, his actions showed quite the opposite. So now what happens? The sun would be setting in mere moments and God was nowhere to be found. The entire day had passed. I had fasted. No one noticed. All the pieces were in place, yet there was absolutely no sign from God. No big revelation. God had been a no-show. Again. How is it possible that He could wake me up three nights in a row, then ask me to fast for a sign He never intended to give me? I wasn't the one responsible for the weird Bible study three nights in a row. I didn't direct myself to the scriptures on fasting and make my own agenda to do it. Heck, I never even put the fasting thing together until the "aha" moment in the tent. None of this made any sense to me at all.

In the near distance I could see Dave's family and the kids gathered there along the cliff's edge. They were facing the water. I wasn't ready to watch the sun go down! *We had an agreement, God! I fasted like you asked me to. You were supposed to answer me. This whole fasting thing was Your idea not mine!* We might have been walking toward the group, but I was a million miles away.

Hearing us approaching behind them, one by one family members turned around to greet us. The closer we got to them, the more their huddle began to separate. Through glimpses, as they began stepping apart, I could see a small table with a white linen cloth covering it. There were roses in a vase. Two champagne glasses sat next to an open bottle. David slowly ushered me toward the setting, then gently motioned for me to sit down in the chair that had been placed there just for me.

Everyone circled around us. Bending down on one knee, he reached into his pocket and pulled out a tiny box. *Oh no! It's happening!!* My mind immediately grasped upward for His heavenly hand. *He's going to propose, and I still don't know what you want me to do! Did you tell me today and somehow, I missed it? I told you I needed a brick in the head to make it clear. What do I do now? I don't know what you want me to say! What do you want me to do?!* The sound of my internal hysterics was muffling David's precious proposal.

He held out the ring. I took it from his hand and squeezed it tightly in the palm of mine. Suddenly everything went into slow motion. The seriousness of the moment overwhelmed me. I couldn't make another mistake. I knew I didn't have God's permission to say yes and with all these people staring at me, I couldn't say no. Unable to speak, I simply leaned forward into David, still kneeling in front of me. Burying my face into his shoulder, I shut my eyes tight. Everyone applauded, but I had not said, "Yes." I knew I couldn't make that commitment until God showed up with that brick.

How was it that I could miss the forest for the trees? Religious rules had so blinded me that I was about to miss this unmerited gift I was so clearly receiving. God's mercy was on display front and center, unfolding in this very moment and I was too focused on the rules to see it!

With my head still on his shoulder and my eyes still closed, I turned my face in the opposite direction, away from the applause and all the happy but misguided faces.

My heart begged one last time, *PLEASE GOD, PLEASE! TELL ME WHAT TO DO!*

I was undone. I had no more words to say. Bravely, I opened my eyes toward the rhythm of the waves. There before me, the fieriest orange sun was now settling in its final moments on top of the blue horizon. The majesty of it took my breath away. Still, I made no connection. It was then, that the breeze came blowing through my soul with its unmistakable whisper, *"My child, you asked for your sign by sunset."*

God wasn't a no-show. He'd heard my prayers all along and His timing was perfect.

God was right there, meeting me at sunset.

# MY STORY

*Slowing Down to Pray & Reflect*

As I read Chapter Four, I was reminded of my own…

When I think about what I just wrote, it makes me feel…

When I pray asking God for direction, He…

When I read the Bible, I see / feel…

I understand His commandments as being…

When I break those commandments or rules, I feel…

How I feel God will react…

The lie I have uncovered about what I expect from God…

# PRAYERS & MEDITATIONS

## *Chapter 4*

For my thoughts are not your thoughts, neither are your ways my ways, declares the Lord. For as the heavens are higher than the earth so are my ways higher than your ways and my thoughts than your thoughts. Isaiah 55:8-9 (ESV)

So we fasted and implored our God for this, and he listened to our entreaty. Ezra 8:23 (ESV)

"Yet even now," declares the LORD, "return to me with all your heart, with fasting, with weeping and with mourning." Joel 2:12 (ESV)

And when you fast, do not look gloomy like the hypocrites, for they disfigure their faces that their fasting may be seen by others. Truly, I say to you, they have received their reward. Matthew 6:16 (ESV)

The Lord is merciful and gracious, slow to anger and abounding in steadfast love. He will not always chide, nor will he keep his anger forever. He does not deal with us according to our sins, nor repay us according to our iniquities. Psalm 103:8-10 (ESV)

As far as the east is from the west, so far does he remove our transgressions from us. Psalm 103:12 (ESV)

As a father shows compassion to his children, so the Lord shows compassion to those who fear him. For he knows our frame, he remembers that we are dust. Psalm 103:13-14 (ESV)

If we confess our sins, he is faithful and just to forgive us our sins and to cleanse us from all unrighteousness. 1 John 1:9 (ESV)

My Prayer…

# Chapter 5

# Meeting
# God in my Fear

*I* had this staggering fear. It was always there, always somehow connecting itself to everything I did. It orchestrated grand worst-case scenarios and petrifying what-if questions that claimed center stage the majority of my life. As far as I could remember, it had always been this way. And the crazy part? All of this was okay with me. It was *normal*. I had come to the false conclusion that playing out fear's dictates in my head somehow made me ready, should a horrible catastrophe ever strike. That way I wouldn't be the one caught off guard. Not me. I'd always have a plan. I'd land on my feet, should it ever happen… which it never did.

Maybe this sadistic practice became a normal part of my life due to being raised in a charismatic church in the middle of the seventies. This was an era that liked to wield the "rapture" sword around like a warrior in the battle of the pews. They did it a lot. No kid I knew in our neighborhood youth group was exempt from the fear of being "left behind."

I can remember coming home from school on a day when my mom should have been there, only to find the house eerily empty. After running room to room, finding each one vacant, the familiar pang would grip my heart. I'd quickly do a mental inventory for any unforgiven sin I might have missed. Had I confessed *everything*? Oh man, was I relieved when finally, I'd catch the faint sound of her muffled voice, and the squeak of the front door opening. I was spared from eternal doom for yet another day. I'd then vow to get my life in order from that point further, profusely thanking Him for the opportunity given. Different versions of "missing the rapture" was commonplace in my earliest years.

Imagine growing up like that? With the very real and constant fear that at any moment you could be permanently ditched by the

Almighty? My young reality was always fused with a theology that demanded I stay on high alert at all times. If I slipped up, even for a moment, that could be the second He came! I would be left on this planet, to await my fate—a biblical proportion of wrath soon to be poured out. All alone, while my Christian friends and family were safely tucked away in heaven, I'd be here, to meet the end of time. I'd be a fugitive on the run, suffering the consequences of my disobedient ways. The crippling fear of all this happening to me was absolutely terrifying to my young and pliable mind.

I'm not saying this doctrine is wrong in its origin. There's definitely biblical truth here. I'm not challenging scripture or trying to instigate a theological debate. The problem I have is when scripture is misused and manipulated to purposefully create fear or confusion in those who hear it. I sat through many a sermon like this and yes, it did its intended job on me. It created a monstrous fear—one I would wrestle with for years. Many of the spiritual leaders of the day used these scare tactics to simply fill the house. This way they could boast growing and even full attendances of those waiting to hear their messages from God. I recall a youth leader subliminally pitching this fear to us young listeners. It went something like this: *If you chose pizza with worldly friends over attending a youth group service and that happens to be the night Jesus came... Well, sorry Charlie. You chose your fate.*

Was this really the gospel Jesus came to give humankind? A gospel of fear? I never stopped to ask myself that question. I wouldn't have known to. I didn't know any better than to do my best to comply. Is it any wonder I had so many issues growing up? This type of preaching fed my biggest mental rival, it fattened and grew my constant yet twisted companion, my terror-gripping fear. They used the big guns on me, and it worked. The grandaddy in the legalist arsenal was effective: God's wrath! Their justification in all of this?

They were scaring us into heaven for our own good. We'd have eternity to work out the details. I guess it's not for me to assume each was coming from this angle, perhaps there were some who truly meant well, even if their methods were off base. But even though others initially spoon-fed this fear to me, later, it would be shoveling it down my own throat. It worked as a terrific self-discipline strategy, a brilliant way to keep myself in line. It was the perfect partner to mingle with my perfectionism. They fit together so nicely.

Sadly, I didn't "learn of God" as the loving Father He says He is. Instead, I learned tactics men created for control, *for their own benefit,* not mine, and certainly not God's. Assuming you've read the earlier chapters, you'll recall the messes this warped theology made, affecting my reasoning and ultimately my life. What's so scary, the very people who touted the answers were the ones who drowned out His voice, the voice He Himself whispered in me when I was so very young. I trusted these spiritual advisors because they were the knowing ones, and I was just a kid. I had a love for God and wanted to be near Him. I turned to them to lead me in the rest. They, in response, stifled the Divine, and replaced Him with their own clanging symbols of arrogance.

Still, miraculously God would not be silenced. Despite their best efforts, He remained in me, even if I couldn't hear Him for a while. He wasn't threatened by their smoke and mirrors. He had a hold on me that ran deeper than any deceiving doctrine that came rolling down the pike. He outlasted the hype and surfaced above the noise. He always made a way through the chaos and found me time and again in the rubble of their madness. He chose me before I ever knew my own name. It was like living a version of that famous movie line, long before my feet ever walked this planet, He had me at hello. Yet, still, I couldn't let go of my love-hate relationship with this implanted fear. It kept some sort of value. Why? What was wrong with me?

Over the years, fear's tentacles seemed to reach and manifest into just about every aspect of my life. The common way it showed itself was through incessant and needless worry. This wasn't a simple worry, like the kind a kid gets after breaking mom's favorite vase or when they get a bad grade on a report card. This was the brutal kind that froze me in its moment. The kind that would lead straight into panic attacks, long before I knew what a panic attack was. Chronic worry was my friendly nemesis. Even as a child, it haunted me, paralyzed me. Yet, I joined it, bullying myself with it. Once when I was in second grade, I recall freaking myself out over the contemplation of Heaven and Hell. Obviously, this was much too vast a topic for a young mind, but that didn't stop me. *What if, in eternity, I was separated from my family? What if some of us went to heaven and others didn't? We would never, ever, EVER see each other again!* Just that thought alone, sent me into hysterics, sobbing to my poor mother who had the unasked-for task of calming me back down again.

Back then, my anxiety level could shoot through the roof, simply by stumbling across an unwanted or unanswerable thought. Pondering negative scenarios like this would send my fear meter pinning the red zone. I could easily become an emotional mess by imagining my worst-case scenarios coming true. It was a toxically draining cycle, for me and for the others who had an unfortunate place in my life.

In time, out of sheer necessity, I forced myself to improve at labeling and masking this fear that held my insides captive. As if hard wired in me, it had a mind of its own. It was an immediate autopilot go-to in any situation where I didn't know the outcome, which was most everything. Oddly, instead of rejecting this emotional yo-yo behavior, I clung to it as if somehow it could save me from the imagined havoc that was coming for me. In fear's iron grip, I wrongly believed if I worried long enough, allowing these scary thoughts to roam back and forth in my head, the answers would surely come and free me from the torment. The more I "cared" about something or someone, the more time I invested worrying about it or them. It felt necessary. Valuable.

I "cared" deeply about many things.

Especially my kids.

Raising four children presented many opportunities for my fear to run rampant. From one having a fever to the another coming in past curfew, I had my worst-case-scenarios drawn up and executed accordingly. But each time, the worries were unfounded and everything would turn out okay in the end. I never was. I hadn't yet connected what a tremendous amount of wasted time and energy was being spent on *nothing.*

The very worst fear I can ever remember, manifested on occasions involving my family, more specifically my kids. Glancing away for a second, then turning back to find one of them missing was always a heart stopper. There's nothing quite like the razor-sharp terror of not being able to locate the back of my kid's head while on a family outing to a crowded amusement park. But then again it could happen while in my own front yard. Whether scanning a sea of strangers, or searching an empty street in my neighborhood, there were many episodes that would find me running all over, yelling their name until I located them. Most of the time they were right there, just out of my immediate sight.

The end of the line, the last straw, came when one of them, my son Zach, "went missing." He wasn't technically lost, but for me, in that horrifying moment, it was as if he was. In the middle of winter, on a white-covered mountainside thick with snow, I couldn't find my son. With a forest full of pines obstructing the view, it was every mother's worst nightmare come true.

All our kids, our two sons especially, were raised snowmobiling. Both boys have ridden since they were able to straddle in front of their dad. With them snugly positioned, whether in front, or tightly holding on behind him, they'd take to the trails, sledding all over the mountain terrains carved near our cabin. Helmet heads bobbling, they'd hang on for dear life, awkwardly gripping the handlebars with their bulky little gloves. When our oldest son, Zach was about nine, he was finally big enough to ride his own snowmobile, instead of having to hop on with his dad. This was a big deal.

One winter morning, a group of us went for a long ride. We'd arrived at a snowy meadow, where we decided to stop and "play" for a bit. This was the time that some in our clan would ride off the groomed trail and cut through fresh powder. Winding around, zig zagging over humps and hills, everyone stayed within close range. We decided to let Zach trail behind his dad and experience this fresh powder firsthand. I stayed at the base of the hill waiting with a few others while they took off to climb it with their sleds. After a short while, one by one, each from our group came circling back where the rest of us were waiting. As I saw Dave approaching, panic immediately struck. Zach was no longer behind him. Nor had he already circled back. Frantically scanning the side of the mountain, Zachary was nowhere in sight. Terror rose in me at warp speed. I felt dizzy. Tears were already stinging my frozen eyelids before anyone said a word. Back and forth and back and forth my eyes searched the area just looking for a glimpse of him. It was as if he had vanished. My fears screamed with everything in me, *Our son is lost!* And the worse part of it was that it appeared he was lost off the trail! I struggled to breathe.

There were so many tracks it was impossible to tell which one would lead to him. My head was spinning with the morbid possibilities. He could have gotten himself backwards, mistakenly heading away from us, deeper into the thick trees. The dreaded worst-case scenario was materializing before my eyes. My husband and a couple of others immediately took action and rerouted back up the side of the hill crisscrossing through the other riders there. After several minutes, that felt like hours, thank God, they found him! Everything was going to be okay. Zach came following them back down the hill and was soon safely back with us. But the *what ifs* continued to knock around inside my head, taking their sweet time to settle down. It made me queasy just thinking about how differently this day could have ended. I praised God for His protection.

That incident shook me awake to a truth buried in me. It was like opening my eyes to find I'd been sitting in a jail cell, handcuffed. That day I became painfully aware that I was, indeed, a literal prisoner of my own fear. Over time, I had slowly allowed simple worry to morph into such an uncontrollable anxiety that now the iron bars were thick and embedded in me. They'd become a part of me. Grooves of fearful auto responses now controlled my every knee-jerk reaction. I was hopelessly bound to repeat these behaviors again and again. Anytime this crippling emotion decided to rear its ugly head, I was its captive. I had given over complete and total control to the intimidation of my fears.

But now I was aware of it. And I didn't like it. This episode with Zach was the end of the line. I'd had enough. I was sick and tired of being led around by this tormenting feeling, loathing how it gripped me each and every time I perceived danger. I hated how quickly it warped my thoughts into raw anguish. It was relentless, banging its lead pipe against the bars of my cell, just to make sure I knew it was there.

Like a tiny key lowered on a golden chain, a question arose out of this aha moment. *If I believe in God and have faith in Him, then why am I always so fearful? What good is faith in my heart, if fear controls my mind? Why have I given place to fear and allowed it to have the upper hand? Isn't God greater than my fear? Do my actions say He is in control or do they not?*

The questions unraveled me. It was frightening to admit that my faith in God usually crumbled and disappeared during times of panic. When the rubber hit the road, my faith was as strong as a backfiring puff of smoke and left me as quickly. My embarrassing prayers, begging Him to take away my threatening circumstances or pleading with Him to make everything okay clearly weren't working. I'd been doing that for years. I was trying to have enough faith yet losing emotional control every time things didn't go the way I felt they should. Fear was sitting in the corner with its arms folded laughing at my flimsy spiritual acts. My faith was borderline comical. It was downright pathetic.

I'd finally grown sick of the circus that fear was making of my life. For the first time I could see the mockery it was creating. It had taken every ounce of my dignity until there was nothing left. I humbly stood stripped of every scrap of pride. I took my barebones honesty straight to the only one who could help. It felt good to come clean with God. I could now see and readily admit it was my hand all along that had been directing this chaos. I was the one creating my own panic! I confessed: no longer did I want to be ruled by fear. Fear would no longer be allowed to be the driving force in my life. I could see the lie for what it was. Fear never served any good purpose, whatsoever. Not even once. Speaking straight into its face I told fear to leave. I didn't NEED it anymore and it was no longer welcome. I knew things were going to change, even if I didn't know how. Fear was all I'd ever known. It's where I resided every time an alarming situation came my way. How would I fight now? How would I walk free from my cell when the feelings banged the bars so strong? I could see my powerlessness. When fear came, though I despised it, I always allowed it to stay. Or more precisely, I always stayed in it. Why? This time I allowed myself to let my prayer be just that, a prayer asking Him to help me in a way that I could not understand. With this, a whole new focus began softly shaping this prayer. I wasn't asking Him to change the circumstances that caused fear to rise, I was asking him to change the way I responded to those situations. I asked this prayer for myself, but really the benefit of it would spill to everyone around me as well.

Understanding the issue didn't create automatic change. Unfortunately, it would be a much more painful process than that. With each step I was willing to take toward it, an altering inside of me was happening as well. Being the one that designed it, I think God had Himself a little fun with how it all came together.

This is the only way I can explain it: After praying, asking God to help me in my crippling fear, it was like I was thrown into the depths of the ocean during the blackest night. Over the next month, three significant scenarios involving close family members would happen. One with my mom, one with my husband and the final one with my daughter. In three unique situations, three separate occasions, each one of them would go missing. What would I do? Was this a mere coincidence? I know it was not.

It was fairly late one evening when I got a phone call. No one knew where mom was. An older woman out late at night? I immediately began to worry, drawing dark conclusions as usual. But right away I noticed something had shifted in me. This time I was aware of what I was doing. Though I was acting in the same fearful way I'd always done, this time it was almost as if I had a front row seat to my own performance. I recognized the chaos in this behavior. But by the time I'd caught it, the emotional train had already left the station and had made its way down the track. It took a while to slow things down from there. It wasn't super pretty but I managed, for the very first time, to slowly turn my focus away from the panic and onto God, even though my anxiety was still clawing toward the roof. That was a brand-new behavior for me. While I was struggling to keep fear's hands off the wheel, my phone rang with the good news, Mom was okay. I sighed a thankful relief for her safety. Strange peace lingered as I whispered gratitude for recognizing the shift that had occurred in me this night.

Round two came about a week later. Typically, when David goes snowmobiling, we have an agreement that he's always off the mountain and calling me by 4:00 pm to check in. This is a safety precaution that we both feel is wise. This particular ride, he and another rider had met up with some others in a backwoods area that had very little trail markings. I was nervous for him to go but trusted his judgment. So, when 4:00 pm came and went with no call, the usual needles of anxiety began to puncture my calm. Where was he? An hour later, still nothing. 5:00 pm dragged into 6:00 pm. Silence. It was now dark outside and I was frantic.

With the valid concerns swirling in my head, I didn't want to think about my behavior this time. I threw out the so-called lesson I'd just learned with my mom's recent episode. This was different. It seemed clear that David had either broken down on the side of the mountain, or was possibly hurt from an accident and unable to get word to me. I told myself I had a good reason to lose it this time.

With inclement weather at hand, there was a real chance he could die out there overnight. My trying to stay positive didn't apply in this scenario. But, each time I wanted to give in to the hysteria, the gentle thoughts would come interrupting, *"Slow down. Breathe. Don't allow panic to grow. Try to remember, God has been showing you that He's here. Trust!"* The words were hard to focus on with fear's screaming siren in my ears. I tried to straighten out my scattering thoughts. I quickly prayed for a mental reset and actively began pushing back against this cycle of fear. I knew I needed to turn away from it and back to trusting the outcome to Him. Though I felt myself losing, I didn't give up. I was determined to stay in the fight. The ringing of my cell phone jarred me out of the mental battle. I grabbed the phone and answered, "Hello???" I heard nothing but a crackling.

His voice finally broke through, but only for a second. I heard him say, "I'm okay" before the call dropped completely. But it was enough to calm me down, just enough to allow me a moment to regain my composure, my focus once more. This time I had stopped and consciously asked for His strength to come and help me fight my fear, but the fight wasn't over yet. It would be another half hour before my phone rang again and I learned the news. Yes, he had gotten stranded on the mountain, but he had managed to make it safely to his truck and was now on his way home! This time the worst-case scenario had its merit, but it was never the whole picture. There was a storm coming, and yes, he was stuck in a snowcovered remote area. What fear had taunted was actually true. BUT, now widening the lens, I could see it was only a *fraction* of the truth. Fear had me glued to the scariest part. So, in the end, what good did giving into fear serve?

Then came the final round. It happened only a few days later. Kristen, our daughter, had recently moved back home to save money. I stood in her doorway as we chatted for a few minutes at the end of the evening. She was in her pajamas, sitting on the edge of her bed. Her blankets were neatly folded back at an angle, with her laptop sitting open there in front of her. When we'd finished talking, I walked over and gave her a kiss then headed to my bed.

The next morning, standing in the kitchen pouring a second cup of coffee, I realized there'd been no sound of stirring in the bedroom above me. I wondered why she was sleeping so late. I popped up the stairs to tap on the door and say good morning. Turning the corner in the hallway I noticed her door was ajar. *That's weird.* I thought. She usually kept her door closed at night. I walked towards her room and pushed the door all the way open. There sat her laptop still on, open on her bed. Her bed, which clearly was never slept in, still had the blankets folded back in the same position they were the night before.

I turned and went back downstairs. Maybe she was in the bathroom, or my room and I'd somehow missed her. Looking around the house, it was clear she wasn't home. I noticed that although I was bewildered, I was calm. I reached for my phone and sent her a quick text. A few minutes went by with no response. After several more minutes passed, I called her. It went straight to voicemail. *Okay. Where is she?* While the minutes stacked up, I was once more aware of what was happening inside me. Despite the strangeness of not being able to find my young adult daughter, I wasn't running around the house in my usual panic. I felt concern of course, but not the over-the-top paralyzing fear I normally would have felt and acted on in this type of situation. Though it made no sense at all that she left the house that night and had yet to return this morning, I would not freak out about it. I would turn my concern instead to prayer and trust God with it, and with her. *Thank you for reminding me that you're in control. You know exactly where she is right now, even if*

*I don't. I trust in you—not in my fear.* This time, I would not allow fear to take the lead. Instead, I had deliberately focused my thoughts on the lessons I'd been learning in the last few weeks and on the only One who could truly help me in the moment.

I was still praying when suddenly, ding! A reply text finally came, "Hi mom." She'd been invited to an overnighter at her friend's house. She'd left late because her friend ran late at work that night. Kristen reminded me that she had mentioned her plans to me the day before. I'd simply forgotten. She was not lost. She was not missing. She was simply waking up and she was just fine.

And for the first time ever, so was I.

I'd met God in my fear and fear lost its tyranny over me.

# MY STORY

*Slowing Down to Pray & Reflect*

As I read Chapter Five, I was reminded of my own…

When I think about what I just wrote, it makes me feel…

If I'm honest with myself, I'll admit I don't want to face my fear of…

The fear I've battled the longest with is…

These fears make me feel…

Fear has already stolen from me in the following ways…

How this fear might shape my future is…

An example of a time when I turned to God in my fear, this happened afterwards…

The lie I have uncovered about my fear is…

# PRAYERS & MEDITATIONS
## *Chapter 5*

So do not fear, for I am with you, do not be dismayed for I am your God. I will strengthen you and help you; I will hold you with my righteous right hand.  Isaiah 41:10 (NIV)

God is our refuge and strength, an ever-present help in trouble. Therefore we will not fear, though the earth give way and the mountains fall into the heart of the sea, though its waters roar and foam and the mountains quake with their surging.  Psalm 46:1-3 (NIV)

For the Spirit God gave us does not make us timid, but gives us power, love and self-discipline.  2 Timothy 1:7 (NIV)

The Lord is my helper, I will not be afraid. What can mere mortals do to me?  Hebrews 13:6 (NIV)

Even though I walk through the darkest valley, I will fear no evil, for you are with me; your rod and your staff, they comfort me. Psalm 23:4 (NIV)

He will cover you with his feathers, and under his wings you will find refuge; his faithfulness will be your shield and rampart. You will not fear the terror of night, nor the arrow that flies by day. Psalm 91:4-5 (NIV)

My Prayer…

# Chapter 6

# Meeting God
# in the Bathroom

*I* wasn't mildly irritated. I was straight-up sulking. I wasn't exactly sure who it was that I was most upset with. Was it Dave? Our friends? Or was it God? Who had caused my frustration? Maybe it was each of them rolled into one. All I knew was that what had just happened was totally unfair. Though I'd been told God never plays "favorites," it sure seemed that way. And from the look of things, my husband was the apple of His Almighty eye. I was clearly last week's tuna.

Let me explain what happened: We'd gone to an event with some good friends. They were the kind of people that made friendship easy. They were the ones we could kick our shoes off with and just be ourselves. From day one, the four of us just seemed to click, effortlessly. By this point we knew each other fairly well and we'd grown to genuinely love them. Leaving their company in a great mood was always a given, so I had no reason to think this time would be any different. But it was. At least for me it was.

In a room full of people, the four of us had migrated toward each other, balancing our drink glasses and platefuls of food. We were happily huddling there with our food when all of a sudden—Bam! It was said. With the flash of a tongue, my appetite completely disappeared, as did my jovial mood. Judging from the look of things, no one else had noticed the quick turn south. Apparently, it was just me.

From the way I'm making this sound, you'd think some horrible insult was hurled in my direction, or at least an ill-timed joke made at my expense… but it was neither. It was nothing like that. There was no rude comment made, in fact, it was quite the opposite. The point in question was the extremely thoughtful and heartfelt compliment that came out of our friend's mouth. What could I find wrong with that? I mean, it was a compliment, for heaven's sake!

What was my issue? Well… I'm gonna tell you. This wonderful thing our friend had just said in the moment, was said *about Dave.* It wasn't said about or in reference to *me.* And that wasn't sitting well with my self-righteous attitude! (Before you judge me, just wait—it gets worse!)

For the rest of that immediate conversation, I just stood there not saying a word. I was too busy pouting. These few innocent sentences between good friends had now lodged sideways in me, in a way that I couldn't describe. The entire vibe of my evening had permanently shifted. I was done here, wanting nothing more than to simply go home. I knew that would only make things worse. Everyone else was having such a wonderful time! How rude and unexplainable would leaving be? I glanced at my watch and began counting minutes until we could graciously exit without too much commotion. It would be a while. I tried to keep my irritation from grimacing my see-through face. That would be a challenge. As I attempted to mask my feelings for the duration of the evening, I found every reply, every smile, every comment to be painfully superficial. Finally, the time came to say goodbye. Without needing my husband's usual coaxing to extract me, I was the first one to the door. Down the walkway and into the car in less than 30 seconds, it was a record! I was more than ready to get away from this whole situation.

Sitting in silence as we pulled out of their neighborhood, I wasn't entirely sure Dave had noticed my off-putting behavior. "What happened? You're so quiet, is something wrong?" he half-asked as he turned onto the main parkway toward home. I'm not sure if he was clueless or just pretending to be. Either way, I had now decided this whole thing was definitely his fault. Blankly staring out my side window, I was not willing to engage nor even toss a glance in his direction. I wasn't sure how to answer his trite question and even if

I did know what to say, I wasn't going to. I had the strong urge to punch him for even asking it. What had happened earlier felt one hundred percent wrong. *Surely, he knew that.* I had been personally slighted. I had been robbed! He'd stolen the praise, and it left me feeling utterly invisible.

Trying to make my words sound better than the crispy reply they were, I softly mumbled, "I just feel… I feel like I deserved that compliment you got tonight." Dave was quiet, so I continued digging myself in a little deeper, "You know what I'm talking about, don't you? Behind closed doors, I'm the one who did the work, not you. They might not have seen it, but you know the truth. And you went ahead and let them compliment *you*! You didn't even acknowledge me in the slightest." My self-pitying voice choked then trailed off for just a moment before circling back yet again, "Why should I even bother? I work so hard to do the right thing, but in the end, you get all the praise. So, why should I continue doing it? What's the point?" Yikes! I'm ashamed to admit I really did say that. It was arrogant and awful, I know.

Of course, he was shocked and immediately insulted by my rude train of thought. My attempting to somehow take credit or outright steal his newly awarded kudos was harsh and out of line. Instead of being happy or proud of him, I'd just used it to crush him big time. It was a bad idea, but by then I was on a roll. I began pulling out a mental list of all the wonderful reasons that I was the real hero here. One by one, I recounted every brownie point that equated to the praise I had so dutifully deserved yet was denied. This was clearly not my shining moment as a wife and he was quick to let me know it. A fight between us was soon ignited. Back and forth, we snipped at the other for the remainder of the drive home. In hindsight, the ridiculousness of us arguing over the ownership of a compliment was completely embarrassing. In this particular case, my obnoxious defense was definitely the weakest.

By the time we pulled into the driveway the infamous compliment lay shredded on the floorboard of the car. The heated darkness of our garage covered us both. The evening and this conversation were more than over. Turning off the engine, Dave sat stoic, frozen in the driver's seat staring at nothing. He was now ignoring me completely. Done with this nonsense, he was done talking to me as well. Furious with being ignored further, I stomped into the house, slamming the door behind me. How could he not see it? Why couldn't he simply acknowledge where I was coming from? What a selfish jerk he was!

If I would have been honest with myself in the moment, I would've had to acknowledge my over-the-top pettiness. That wasn't going to happen. I couldn't see past my own wounded pride to admit *anything*. My behavior wasn't right in the least, but that didn't stop the intense feelings of resentment from seething inside of me. That night was proving something that I'd suspected for a long time. I was invisible. I had to say something to keep from disappearing all together. To me, this evening was a testimony to the fact that *no one really saw me at all.*

Why did I feel so invisible? So insignificant? So erasable?

Any way you look at it, what happened that evening wasn't Dave's fault. It wasn't our friend's fault either. And God had nothing to do with it. The drama was all mine. Even the fight that occurred after we'd left their house that night was started by my own sharp tone reflecting nothing but my insecurities. I was jealous, plain and simple. I was self-focused and unbending. This wasn't pretty on any scale. Now I was paying the price, I was sitting alone. There on my bedroom floor, I caught my own reflection in the mirror. I was a hot mess. The smeared mascara might have been everywhere on my face, but the distractions were all gone. The heat of the moment had finally dissipated, and I had calmed down. Now, as I sat reflecting on my erratic behavior, I searched for a reason, other than blame, for why it happened. Why did tonight's situation upset me so much? And why did my attitude turn so hateful so quickly toward those I cared for most? Surely, these friends cared for me as much as I did them. I wasn't invisible in their eyes. So why did I respond that way?

*What do others see that I don't see? Do they think I'm self-absorbed? Arrogant? Do I think I deserve special treatment or an award? Am I a blind hypocrite?* I tried to poke around in my own soul for a response. Though genuinely asking, the questions seemed hollow and without answers. An arrogant person knows they're arrogant right? Doesn't a hypocrite know exactly what they are? These types of people use smoke and mirrors to create false images to extract praise from those around them. That wasn't me. I would never do that. That wasn't at all how I felt. I wasn't seeking mere attention nor adoration from our friends. Or was I? Maybe I was blindly fooling myself?

Our deepest beliefs bleed out through our actions. I had to admit, I hadn't liked my actions for a very long time. Especially that night. So maybe, yes. Maybe, I was the one who couldn't see. If so, where was the disconnect? I was far too familiar with the feelings of embarrassment and regret that came after my tirades. Often, I'd behaved contrary to what I professed to believe. I was, in many ways, a walking contradiction. I imagined everyone else around me must have noticed that as well. Why couldn't I connect the dots?

I didn't understand my own behavior, but I knew one thing. I was sick of it. I could see my own impatience; how overly critical I had become over the years. If I wasn't gelling with my own actions, it made sense that others disliked them as well. When did my heart grow cold? Was my life now emulating this ice?

If I look in the mirror and don't like what I see, what does this mean?

I mused, sarcastically, maybe the issue was I didn't love myself enough. I'd read the self-love captions on the magazines in the grocery store line. Talk shows were saturated with interviews by experts on the subject. Back then, "Being your own best friend before you can be a friend to others," was the hottest new concept. I considered it, for two seconds. Then I rejected it. Feeling negative about my life because I didn't feel great about myself, seemed like a cop out. Give myself some love? Give me a break. Accepting one's imperfect flaws as loveliness might be what all the self-help books were touting, but I twisted the concept against itself as irresponsible. Of course I did. A royal critic allows no slack—ever! They're too busy keeping score.

But what if I was wrong? What if God was more laid back than I gave him credit for? Like a surfer-dude in the sky, was He hanging out just waiting to give me a big celestial hug, while sending His heavenly love mantras? *"Chill out, my child. It's all good. Mellow now and just relax."* Yeah. I wished it could be that easy. Who wouldn't love to stop and sip on some spiritual umbrella drink, blissfully forgetting about the consequences of their actions? For me, these positive-vibe notions were equivalent to paddling a board out during a tsunami. I would be surfing myself right into destruction. Who's really fooling themselves here? What a responsibility-dodging way to exist. In my mind, this type of *love covers all* mentality was a weak and flimsy answer. My heart wasn't buying it in the least.

A few days after our argument I was getting ready for work, and I had just refilled my cup and was headed to my bedroom. Setting the cup on the counter, I stepped into the shower. I felt the usual uneasiness coming over me. My thoughts had turned to the full day ahead of me and it felt unbearably heavy. I recognized that I'd been having this same feeling not just recently but for several months now. It was like a cloud that would come and hover over me. It was threatening. Ominous. I was my least favorite companion by this point, and just wanted to lose myself in the business of work. And now I had this extra hurdle. The idea of spending another day being "me" seemed unbearable. It had become exhausting just trying to carry out the simplest tasks. My relationship with my clients, that I had once looked forward to and enjoyed, now felt pressing, and at times, overwhelming. I knew my life was near the breaking point. For much too long I had been slowly working my way into a corner with no escape. I knew I had to change, but how to get there remained a mystery to me.

So, there I was, that morning, standing in the shower with the water spraying down on my head. With all roads exhausted, I decided to take the matter up with God. I was worn out from all the trying. Trying to get it right, yet continually falling so blaringly short. In silent desperation, I turned my hopelessness into a prayer. I asked Him if He could tell me what was wrong, more specifically, what was wrong *with me*? How could I remove something that I couldn't see? I confessed that I hated the way I'd been acting, and I was pretty sure He did too. I didn't understand this critical nature inside me. It was growing increasingly caustic as each day passed. I came clean and acknowledged that even if He loved me, I genuinely didn't. And being honest, I admitted that I wasn't entirely convinced that He did either. I concluded by tying all of this together with the simple strand of a childlike request, *Can you please help me?*

That morning, I let go and offered up my feeble yet sincere prayer. With that, I stepped out of the shower and reached for the nearby towel hanging close by. I decided that morning to leave my prayer there—with God. I knew I was out of options anyway. Wrapping the towel around my head, I turned my focus to the hands on the clock.

I don't know exactly what I expected to happen next. Perhaps a new zest for life would burst forth inside me or some incredible sense of patience for myself and others would wash over me, somehow. I didn't feel anything at that moment, but since I was running a bit behind, my thoughts about the prayer took a backseat as I pulled open the drawer and grabbed the blow-dryer.

Just a few minutes into drying my hair, my absentminded gaze floated across the room then steadily fixed on a familiar image that hung on my bathroom wall. It was a thinly framed oblong poster of a printed scripture: 1 Corinthians 13. I'd hung it there years ago. I loved it from the moment I spotted it in a cardboard drugstore display. It wasn't fancy or costly by any means, but there was something special about it that caught my eye and I bought it. It moved with us from our last home, where it had hung proudly and now had its place in this one. So very ordinary, it was something I took for granted as I passed by it day after day. This particular morning, here it was, front and center and commanding my full attention. As I stared at it, for a moment time seemed to stand still. It was as if the words from the print were jumping right out of the frame and into my face! I couldn't ignore what was happening had I tried.

The best way I can describe it is this: it was as if God was speaking to me in 3D. I was reading the verses and they were speaking back to my heart! It was like I was seeing them for the very first time. Every line was exploding with meaning *just for me*. Like beams shooting straight into me, each word reached deep touching the eternal inside. And as crazy as it sounds, in that moment every word was clear, making perfect sense.

For those of you not familiar with this chapter, here's what it says:

Love is patient and kind; Love does not envy or boast;

It is not arrogant or rude.

It does not insist on its own way;

It is not irritable or resentful;

It does not rejoice at wrongdoing, but rejoices with the truth.

Love bears all things, believes all things, hopes all things, endures all things.

Three things last forever…

Faith, hope and love.

The greatest of these is love.

*Boom!* With my hair still damp, I clicked off the dryer, slowly setting it down next to me, without moving my eyes off the narrow frame's message. I stood there marveling at what was happening.

My heart raced while re-reading every line. Leaning in, I was finding myself being pulled closer. Innately sensing this moment was sacred, I carefully raised my hand toward it to connect with what I was reading. Gently, I pressed my index finger against the glass, tracing over each word, taking in each line, as it formed new meaning in me. Then I began searching each row, looking for traces of myself in the string of words. For a moment, I felt a twinge of fear, as I couldn't find anything written there that resembled *me*, or my life. What I mean is, I didn't see anything in what I was reading there that I recognized to be evident in my own life. I only saw what I was not.

What I saw written there was the complete opposite of *me*.

**Love is patient and kind.** *I wasn't patient, I was impatient most of the time.*

**Love does not envy or boast.** *I was envious and jealous. I boasted of my accomplishments. I wanted the praise.*

**It is not arrogant or rude.** *I had been arrogant. I'd felt justified for those times I'd been rude. I was merely defending my cause.*

**It does not insist on its own way.** *I wanted my own way and harbored a cargo ship of resentment.*

**It is not irritable or resentful.** *Clearly, my actions from the previous night (with my friends and Dave) proved I behaved differently.*

**It does not rejoice at wrongdoing but rejoices with the truth**. *My twisted understanding of the truth kept me in a mindset that I was the one being wronged.*

The words flowed, like warm, thick honey filling the holes in my thirsty soul.

The meaning was without question. I finally understood.

*The answer was LOVE. I didn't have love! Not this kind.*

What I saw for the first time was this love, this perfection, was completely encompassed in Him. It was His heart. His perfection. Not mine.

I saw LOVE.

As I looked up toward heaven, the moment was interrupted by the clock that hung high above my head. I was now running very late. But, still, I couldn't help lingering. I wanted to remain there for just one second more. Everything was hinging on the whisper that came next, *"What will you do with what you've been given?"*

My response was as quick as the blow-dryer's switch I'd flicked back on.

As amazingly incredible as it was to receive this ah-ha moment from above, it seemed just as simple to know what I must do next. So, I responded just as naturally, *God, I see it now. I see what's missing. I don't have YOUR love. Please make me like this… (I pointed to the scripture there on the wall) …and please strip from me everything that's in the way of it. Amen.*

It seemed like a completely reasonable prayer—one I meant with total sincerity. I finished brushing my hair, slipped on my dress and shoes, and left for work with a new bounce in my step. Something had just happened. I *knew* it.

It would take time to notice the subtle shifts taking place, but changes were indeed coming. A beautifully terrifying coming undone had slowly begun to unfold inside me.

That morning God heard and answered me.

He'd simply pointed out what had been there all along.

God met me in my bathroom.

# MY STORY

*Slowing Down to Pray & Reflect*

As I read Chapter Six, I was reminded of my own…

When I think about what I just wrote, it makes me feel…

When it comes to others, I can feel invisible when…

I tend to blame *who* for my unhappiness…

When I look in the mirror, do I like what I see? What I see is…

My honest definition of love is…

In what ways does my definition match / clash with the one in 1 Corinthians 13?

I see / do not see this love in me in the following ways…

I see / do not see this love in the following ways I treat others…

The lie I have uncovered about love is…

# PRAYERS & MEDITATIONS

## Chapter 6

He has shown you, O mortal, what is good. And what does the LORD require of you? To act justly and to love mercy and to walk humbly with your God. Micah 6:8 (NIV)

Love is patient, love is kind. It does not envy, it does not boast, it is not proud. It does not dishonor others, it is not self-seeking, it is not easily angered, it keeps no record of wrongs. Love does not delight in evil, but rejoices with the truth. It always protects, always trusts, always hopes, always perseveres. 1 Corinthians 13: 4-7 (NIV)

Therefore, as we have opportunity, let us do good to all people, especially to those who belong to the family of believers. Galatians 6:10 (NIV)

As God's chosen people, holy and dearly loved, clothe yourselves with compassion, kindness, humility, gentleness and patience. Colossians 3:12 (NIV)

Do nothing out of selfish ambition or vain conceit. Rather in humility value others above yourselves, not looking to your own interests but each of you to the interests of others. Philippians 2:3-4 (NIV)

Love must be sincere. Hate what is evil; cling to what is good. Be devoted to one another in love. Honor one another above yourselves. Romans 12:9-10 (NIV)

My Prayer…

# Chapter 7

# Meeting God in my Sadness

*W*e've all heard the phrase, "Admitting you have a problem is the first step toward authentic change." While this may be true, what happens when the first step is the only step you ever take? When you find you're knee deep stuck someplace between the knowing and the doing. What then? That's where I found myself. Hope had slowly dissolved into disappointment. Instead of repelling me away from my undesired traits, the sour smell of self-derogation only added a constant reminder of my failures.

When one slows down enough to humbly accept and admit their flaws, all applaud such a refreshingly brave stand. But, when the standing turns to sitting, and the sitting turns to lying in it once more, well, that's another story. A revelation without change is like whistling in the wind. It's a nice sentiment on the lips but futile when facing a blasting gale.

That was me whistling in the howling wind while the gray clouds continued to hover and settle over my heart. Though I was trying, the number of things I shouldn't have said or done continued piling up. I'd been kidding myself. I would never *really* change. Knowing what was missing in my behavior, yet not finding a way to manifest it felt like a complete joke. My track record for failure and continued dissatisfaction with my own actions was at an all-time high. I had not moved forward. I had not moved at all. In fact, I'd been in this place so long, I'd grown roots! A garden junkyard of negative thoughts and feelings had taken over every nook and cranny of my mind's acreage. I'd become so very tired in this place. Eventually, I gave in to its heavy embrace and danced with its whispered notion of my nothingness.

Through my unshakable sadness, I still managed breathing, despite the constant pressure squeezing my chest in two. The slight breath of hope had grown incredibly faint. That is until the final blow came, smothering any vapor that might be left inside me.

Someone I deeply cared for decided that now would be the perfect time to tell me, with razor-sharp and poignant words, just exactly what he thought of me. It wasn't good. His harsh insinuations made toward me attacked my character, my very identity. His message came as one of total disdain, not merely for my actions, but for the entire Teri Brinsley package as a whole. At least that's how it felt.

To say I was taken aback would've been an understatement. My inner self curled like an unborn fetus around the verbal gut punch of his hurled accusations. All air left my lungs, making me mute, unable to speak a syllable in response. There was clearly no point. His mind had already been made up. I'd been tried, convicted, and sentenced without even knowing I'd been standing in his courtroom. Now, there was nothing I could say or do to change any of it. The stone of division between us had been carved deeply. This event caused the chasm of my sadness to widen ten-fold. It wrecked me. It had the opposite effect on this once-treasured person. He was sighing an enormous relief, at having pushed the weight of me from his life. In the moment of this realization, feeling the worst kind of horrible, as if on cue, the cherry on top of my self-hated behaviors chimed in… *I began to cry.* I had no pride left. I felt such pain, embarrassment and shame as his words continued to echo in my head.

Even the most stench-filled bag of trash is bundled up and tied. It's taken outside and dumped in a place all garbage must go. I now felt lower than that black plastic bag of garbage. Worse than that, I had not even the simple dignity of a twist-tied top. I wasn't tidy, nor was I in my proper place. I'd now come completely undone, spilling out my emotional foulness in every direction.

In addition to what was said of me, or to me, something more troubled me. It was the powerlessness I felt against his cruelty. I was completely vulnerable to the stinging, or should I say bludgeoning of his words. Why was that? Why couldn't I simply dismiss his actions, disassociating from the negativity, and move on? I knew I was far from perfect and readily accepted constructive criticism. I don't dodge accountability. But this wasn't that. What happened wasn't brought to me in light of self-improvement. Had that been the case, I might not have liked what he said but I would've received it and reflected on it, in a healthy way. No, this was a direct attack, a hurtful power jab. It came from a deliberately jaded and misaligned view of me. He *wanted to* think poorly of me, I could see that. So why and how did this biased opinion hold that much power over me? Why did I give it such credence?

The answer wasn't rocket science. It was childishly simple. It was because I *cared.* I loved him and that made me vulnerable.

This person mattered a great deal to me. His words carried tremendous weight in my eyes. They had value. If I didn't love this person, what he said could have bounced right off my thicker skin. The warped image he portrayed of me was far from the person I saw in the mirror every day. I saw no connection, it was too grotesque.

Yet, in that moment I knew I had to stop and honestly take a hard look at myself. With such strong accusations, how could I not do a double then a triple take in the mirror? It was my responsibility to do at least that much. To be fair, I knew I must consider all that was said—whether I initially believed it or not. So, I asked myself, *Am I the person he says I am? Do I behave the way he described? Do I just not see it or am I choosing to ignore such an ugly side of myself?* What a tragic thought! I contemplated it quite seriously.

Whether there was truth to what he said, or whether it was simply meant to wound, here's the bottom line… Does another's negative view prevail over my own unseen intentions? And where does my responsibility lie? Do others have the right to make external judgments and commentaries regarding me and my actions, without having the ability to see into my heart and know why I do what I do? Dare they attempt to label me strictly by my behaviors, using them as the supreme definition of who I really am?

I don't know if you're like me on this, but I have a hard time with someone misjudging me or attempting to name the intentions behind my actions. When I'm coming from a good place, and someone deliberately pollutes it with labeling or finger-pointing, it's incredibly frustrating to say the least. Yet, at times, I'm guilty of doing the same thing to others.

What's wrong with us humans? Why can't so many of us simply decide beforehand to believe the best, regardless of what it might look like on the surface? Why do we so easily bend toward our own negative suspicions? Why is it so tempting to throw another under the bus, quickly and presumptuously accusing them before we'll ever consider giving them the slightest benefit of doubt?

Even if someone blatantly and repetitively behaves badly, in a manner that we find particularly offensive, does that give us the right to name the driving force behind their actions? Do we really know why they do what they do? Hardly. We have no idea what's hidden in that frame. Behind those eyes could be a driving wound—one we could never comprehend. We have no idea what causes people to behave in self-protective ways. We simply don't understand, even if we arrogantly believe we do. Why won't we stop to consider this truth before sizing others up or sadly tossing them aside? What sort of self-adulation are we grasping for when we choose to push another down so that we might stand on top of them to stretch ourselves a little bit higher? Standing on another's neck doesn't make us powerful, it makes us pathetic. It's wreaking arrogance at its finest.

What about the way we talk to ourselves, the internal dialogues between our ears? Those harsh words I speak to myself are things I would never say to another person. Walking around inside this body, I am quite aware of my every flaw. I point them out to myself regularly. I've paced every inch of the distance between who I am and who I desire to be. And when I make mistakes, you can be sure I'll be first in line to point it out, chastising myself. There's a very real tyrant knocking around inside me, and she's counting the minutes until my next failure.

So what about extending grace? Grace for others? Grace for ourselves? Where's my golden-rule patience when someone makes a mistake? Am I any better than they? Regarding judging others, who died and made me their ruler? Why is it that I can be so quick to kick them when they're down? I may not say it, but sometimes I think it. Why is it so tempting to lean in and listen to the down and dirty, but when there's good to share, I've sometimes bitten my lip in silence. I'm dragging out my internal comparison sheet first. I need to be sure I've got more points before I'll toss them my gratuitous compliment or approval. It's when they move too far ahead of me that I become increasingly uncomfortable, desiring to adjust things back into my favor.

If this isn't true of you, then I'm in awe of your restraint. Congratulations. You've achieved a higher level of self-acceptance than I've managed to obtain just yet. Because, if I'm honest, there's still those times when I can see these unsightly actions coming out of me. I'm not proud of it, I hate it, actually. Yet, on the flipside, when someone does it to me, I'm off to the races internally ranting the injustice! When I feel something isn't fair, I can't seem to let it go. And I know this is exactly what happened recently with this person I cared about. It wasn't fair of them to judge me so harshly, so wrongly. Once the boiling emotions of that moment subsided, the pain from it remained. The anchor of sadness refused to leave my soul.

I hate being called "emotional." I despise that label. It's up there with four-letter-words as far I'm concerned. It's extremely condescending and it makes me feel degradingly low, adolescent. Yet, I've heard it spoken of me more than once, by more than one person! I can't argue with the fact that I feel things deeply. Maybe even more than the average person. Can I control what I feel? Is it childish when those feelings get hurt? Or, is it a sign of simply being thin skinned? Maybe so. But I'd rather be clothed with skin that can feel than be covered in a coarse leather that no touch can penetrate. Still, how does one save a tender heart from being beaten up in the process? Certainly, I don't want my feeling heart turning to stone out of self-preservation.

Years ago, when I was struggling with a friendship, for moral support I decided to confide in my sister-in-law, Maria. It was her Divinely inspired words that changed my trajectory on the issue at the time. I still recall what she said, "Your problem is in the expectations you set for others. When you choose to focus on what you're not getting, you can't help but become resentful." She was right! I had been expecting others to act in ways I would have chosen to act had the tables been reversed. When I compared another's choices to what I would've chosen to do, I was appointing myself their judge and jury. At the time, I had repeatedly been setting the bar unrealistically high and it continued leading to problems in my relationships. My pain only served to fuel this unhealthy cycle. I'd been busy sizing others up and passing out verdicts before they'd ever known they were in my courtroom!

Now, as I reflected on that conversation from years ago, I realized there were times my actions had been no better than this person's recent actions against me.

Here I was, nursing a wound that in essence was not far from any I had given to others at some point. I could see it. I could accept it, but what would I do about it? Like so many times before, would I do nothing different with this revelation I'd been given? I knew it was a choice. *I would do something different this time and I would do it right now.* There was no need to wait for the painful feelings to subside before taking a step. All along it had been an illusion that I could do nothing about my situation. It was untrue that I was stuck in this place. This time, reaching beyond my sadness, I began to pick out the tiny glass shards left from those words that slashed my heart. I chose to pour healing grace into those wounded places. I no longer had to guess at their motives. It no longer held relevance for my healing. Another person's choices were never mine to carry. I would no longer mentally examine nor debate any of this. I was now looking through fresh eyes, even while pain still lingered behind them. I chose to let go.

Ultimately, the person responsible for moving past my pain was me!

It didn't happen overnight, but after this awareness, each time I felt the urge to act on those feelings that lingered, I'd stop and reposition my focus. It turns out my unshakable sadness wasn't unshakable after all. It was hanging onto me until I could recognize what was tethered underneath. Below my lingering pain I recognized that my heart wasn't just sad, it was mourning. I wasn't a victim. I was grieving a loss. My heart felt the loss of a relationship with someone

I loved. This sadness wouldn't leave me until I could give in and admit the love I still carried for this person, despite my blinding pain. This love was no longer chained to their reciprocation. It was given freely, without strings. In my heart, love simply existed. I had let go of my right to be upset if I was going to find my way through to the forgiveness this unconditional love offered.

Loving this person, despite their wounding, didn't mean I was saying what happened was okay, nor that we would continue the relationship as before. No. This love existed outside of that, outside my own frail human emotions. God was holding my heart, helping me stand, then move forward, with or without this person in my life. All I had to do was ask Him to unblock the flow. His love moving through me would change everything. When I could see this, even though loss had clearly happened, my sadness, my mourning eventually turned to gratitude. I was now taking brave steps forward in the Divine love that indeed conquers all.

The answer came, not in judgment, but in love… when God met me in my sadness.

# MY STORY

*Slowing Down to Pray & Reflect*

As I read Chapter Seven, I was reminded of my own…

When I think about what I just wrote, it makes me feel…

The strongest negative emotion I see in me most often is…

Deep down, I know I need change in my behavior regarding…

The words said to me that hurt me the most…

I can't let go of the pain they caused because…

The person who hurt me most is…

I struggle to forgive them because…

I let my emotions take the wheel when I…

The lie I have uncovered about my pain is…

# PRAYERS & MEDITATIONS

## *Chapter 7*

Why, my soul, are you downcast? Why so disturbed within me? Put your hope in God, for I will yet praise him, my Savior and my God. Psalm 43:5 (NIV)

Do not be afraid of them, the LORD your God himself will fight for you. Deuteronomy 3:22 (NIV)

Though an army besiege me, my heart will not fear, though war break out against me, even then I will be confident. Psalm 27:3 (NIV)

He will wipe every tear from their eyes. There will be no more death or mourning or crying or pain, for the old order of things has passed away. Revelation 21:4 (NIV)

Cast all your anxiety on him because he cares for you. 1 Peter 5:7 (NIV)

But love your enemies, do good to them, and lend to them without expecting to get anything back. Then your reward will be great, and you will be children of the Most High, because he is kind to the ungrateful and wicked. Luke 6:35 (NIV)

Be kind to one another, tenderhearted, forgiving one another as God in Christ forgave you. Ephesians 4:32 (ESV)

My Prayer…

# Chapter 8

# MEETING GOD IN MY REJECTION

Who am I?

Am I defined merely by a name given to me at birth? What about the roles I play in life? Surely my professional career has something to do with my identity, considering all the years I've spent building it. Or is it more personal than that? Is it how I'm seen in a family; who I'm married to, or that I am married at all? My kids and grandkids, as wonderful as they are, do they define me? And what about wealth? A bulging bank account surely plays a role in naming my personal worth. Yes? Some think so. I'm sure there's as many different answers for this soul-searching question as there are individuals who ask it. Unlike many others, inside me, the familiar mantra nagged, "Who am I… *really?*"

Well, if I don't know the answer, who does?

I'm sure if I'd ask around, a few fine folks will gladly share their niceties of me, of who they believe me to be. But then again, there's probably a surly handful, who have their negative assumptions as well and would judgingly share them accordingly. Can the verbal painting of another's brushstrokes ever be trusted as the canvas for what makes me, *me*?

It would be a crazy ride to base my identity on other's evaluations, especially when they're contradictory! I'd be elevated one minute and cast down the next, everything in me, about me, up for grabs. Would it be so wrong then, to choose to believe only the good said about me? Will this help me know and love myself better? It certainly would make it easier for me to stay in a positive-cocooned frame of mind. Only listening to the positive about myself has the lure of keeping my mind "healthy," but even if I tried to embrace nothing less, it would only take a quick introspective glimpse to negate it all.

I'm my own worst critic, knowing my lengthy list of failings, my repetitive tendencies toward mistakes. This is why it's extremely hard to shake off the negative labels others slap across my forehead. Inside me somewhere, I tend to agree with them. The positive comments, like fluttering butterflies, are elating but fleeting while the negative ones sink in. Like rusty old fishhooks, lodging deep, they fester in my memory. Does the old proverb's wisdom ring true? Am I blind to the majesty of the forest due to the massive number of trees in my view? Maybe. All I know is that those trees have their opinions and love to voice them regularly!

*Am I who others say I am?*

People can be truly kind. They can also be petty, jealous and overtly rude. Should I waste a moment of my time mulling over negative statements that are nothing more than the reflections of another's manifesting insecurities? If it's coming from a dysfunctional place, I should know there is no authentic basis for concern at my end. I am neither responsible nor accountable for another's unhealthy habit. However, in an effort to remain open minded, I'm often torn, conflicted when I analyze comments made toward me. One moment, with the drop of a phrase, I can feel like the entire world is against me. In those moments it seems no one on the planet realizes my true intentions. Yet, in the next moment I'm pummeled into agreeing with their cruel logic, certain that the error lies somewhere within me. I'll take full blame. With that, the self-chastisement begins. *If only I would have done this differently or not said that—everything would have been okay. It's my fault things are the way they are. In the end I always screw things up.*

Could it be true that I create my own chaos? Is it merely the result of my own destructive choices that cause me to be left out in the cold? Is this why I often find myself alone in a crowd? Have I brought this rejection upon myself? Am I purposely, rightfully *forgotten*? I feel it would be foolish not to look deeper at this chilling question.

Some days it feels overwhelming to think that possibly it's true. I deserve what I get. If I follow this path, these thoughts will quickly turn darker, reminding me that it will always be this way. The volume cranks six notches as my internal cynic's voice blasts, *You'll never learn.* The familiar warped truth presses its mark deeper each time, into my brain making sure I never forget it. This mindset unlatches and opens the door to other similar beliefs like, *You'll never get it together. Why keep trying? In the end it always turns out the same. You will somehow alienate them. You are not, nor will you ever be worthy of anyone's time or affection.*

I know entertaining and dwelling on thoughts like this is unhealthy. Of course, I fight against it. I make my plans for change despite their clamoring. That is, until the next time I make a mess of things. It's then, these words spring back to life, smirking their truth in my face. I find, after all my efforts, my striving to do better, my carefulness, after everything, nothing really changes. It always ends the same. I do not feel loved. I do not feel accepted. I feel but one feeling: I feel incredibly alone. And worse, I know I am the one to blame.

This is where I made my bed. I slept in this truth.

In my childhood home, my two older brothers shared a bedroom and like most families, so did my parents. Down our humbly narrow hallway, there were three doors in a row and one tiny bathroom at the end of the hall. My room was sandwiched between my parents' room and my brothers' room. I can remember my preschool self at bedtime each evening. As I lay there in the darkness, my family's voices drifted through the night air, bringing me a sense of peace.

Through the paper-thin walls, their laughter or whispering conversations lulled me to sleep. But something else was happening during that time. Hearing them night after night also created a painful awareness in my young mind. While on either side of me, two people shared their rooms through the night, I lay there in my mine, very much alone.

Looking back at that time in life now from my adult perspective, I'm sure not all of what I heard on each side of me during those sleepy evenings was the merry bliss my young mind thought it to be. But the feelings of a little girl, night after night, alone in the dark, altered something deep inside me. Starting way back then, the weed of a message found its roots in my soul: *You are alone. Even in your own family, you are alone. There is a reason why, you know. The reason, the problem—is YOU.* With time, the tentacles of this belief became woven into my bedrock of learned truths. Not knowing any better, I allowed myself to be absorbed by it. In time, much of who I was disappeared into the fog of its implied meaning. I become a ghostly version of myself.

Whether it's self-inflicted or beyond our control, perceived or actual, rejection messes with us on such a deep level that we'll do just about anything not to feel discarded or invisible. We become people pleasers, waiting for the next fix of another's approval. Or we'll strive to be perfect, with a mentality that somehow we'll control their possible rejection, by walking that flawless line. Or worst of all, we'll beat rejection to the punch by becoming a recluse. Our reasoning makes sense, we won't be abandoned by others if they never have the chance. As a result, we cut off all roads that would lead us into relationship and connection, in a constant effort to avoid all possibility of pain that could be lurking therein.

Over the course of my life, I've tried on all these behavioral shoes. As the years went by, I found all I ever gained was cramped toes and blistered feet. None of them were comfortable in the least, let alone able to truly improve or change anything about my life. These fix-myself behaviors only left me more broken, more frustrated, more alone. Instead of any cure or relief, walking around in these false beliefs created a continuing spiral of self-defeat. I had little tolerance for my own stumblings, and less for anyone who was near enough to point at my feet. Hobbling down life's road, wearing the shoes of people-pleasing, perfectionism and self-isolation never took me where I wanted to go. They never delivered the hope they promised. They never met the lingering needs that remained deep inside me. Instead, they distorted and magnified them. They mocked them. All of them. My need to belong, my need to be valued and my need to be accepted in my imperfectness. My insatiable need to be loved. I felt pathetic. *How could I be so needy? So weak?*

Like a triathlete with no finish line, I ran with everything in me faster and ever forwards, chasing my own elusive brokenness, determined to put an end to it, yet never getting anywhere on its circular track. No matter how hard I tried, I'd always end up right back in the place I'd started. Alone. Each time I got back up a little more scraped, a little more bruised and immensely more bitter. Eventually, after so many attempts and repeated failures, I slowly lost my grip on hope. Exhausted, I came to my end and then gave in to it. I accepted the truth ringing in my ears. It would be a relief to just be done with it. Laying down my fight, I numbly joined the crowd of voices in my head.

Finally, it was done… I rejected *me*.

I used to have a recurring dream. There were different scenarios, but always the same theme, I was being chased. I would desperately try to run, but my lead-filled legs would barely move. The effort was there, but I would be close to paralyzed in place. No matter how hard I tried to get away, the ominous would be closing in on me. In the end, right before I was caught, I'd always wake up, heart pounding so loudly I could hear it.

Then one night, the dream was defilingly different. So different that I never forgot it. Little did I know at the time, the details of this dream would become life altering.

The dream was as dark visually as was its scenario. It began with me behind the wheel of my then-owned car. I was racing up a two-lane road late at night. As the scene unfolded, I was being chased by a threatening thunderstorm. While in this state of panic, I looked over to my right. There, buckled in the passenger seat next me, a young girl sat silently. She was seemingly unaware of my anxious mental state. Instead, she sat emotionless, facing straight ahead as I drove.

The road in front of us was leading up an incredibly steep mountain. Looking back over my shoulder, through the rear window I could see the violent storm clouds swirling. They were moving closer. I tightened my grip around the wheel and pushed the gas pedal to the floor. With no fear of speed, I used everything in me to distance us from this impending doom. Higher and higher my car ascended up the grade. The farther up the mountain we climbed, the narrower the road became. Within seconds, this two-lane road had become one marginal lane. With every blink the sides of the road were coming closer in on us, until ultimately bringing the road to an end, to a literal point. I could drive no further. The jarring cliffs clawed on either side.

Despite the blackness of night and the howling wind, the decision was made. We couldn't stay here and allow the storm to overtake us. We had no choice but to leave the vehicle. Without much thought, I swung my door open, stepped outside and peered over the cliff's edge. The young girl did the same, following close behind me. We stood together, there in the darkness, with barreling black clouds breathing in. There was nowhere left to go. The mist of the storm was almost breathable at this point. It was inches away. We would soon be consumed by this thundering storm unless…. Unless we did the impossible: We would have to go over the edge!

I stooped down to a sitting position along the cliff's edge. As I carefully swung both legs over, they disappeared into the weightlessness of the foggy black night. The jagged edges pushed into the backs of my knees as I slowly lowered myself off the ledge. Once over, I'd managed somehow to secure a holding through the loose dirt, finding solid stone beneath. With the weight of my entire body now descended, I was completely relying on the firm rock underneath my hands. Again next to me, amazingly, the young girl hung there doing just the same.

Together, we slowly began scaling, inch by inch, back down the rocky incline. Interestingly, the storm didn't seem to be following us now. Instead, it remained up on the road by the car. With feet dangling miles above the ground, the stone mountain edge we clung to began to morph in color and texture. Slowly, beneath us, as we moved along, the rocky cliffside itself began to change into giant puzzle pieces. Interestingly the puzzle pieces were an assortment of distinct colors and instead of a hard jagged rock, the stone wall had turned into a velcro-type texture. I knew what that meant. In that moment, I took it to imply that every color had a different meaning, but that all were connected and equally important. Each piece being part of the next, all were necessary to create a whole picture. We would have to make our way past them all if we were to find our sure footing again.

Just as this realization hit me, a dark figure appeared out of nowhere. Suddenly, he was right there hanging on the cliff next to us! This threatening dark-cloaked man was intently pursuing me. Another chase had begun.

Staying focused on my grip and not the evil presence next to us, I continued to move down the side of the mountain with the young girl mirroring my every move. The dark figure continued to move closer with every moment. Finally, I came to a place where I found the strength to swing one leg up and over enough to slowly pull myself back over the ledge to a point of safety. Standing on two feet, my young female companion was right there alongside me.

Just as I thought we had finally outrun this threat, the dark-cloaked figure leapt up from over the edge and grabbed toward me. But this time I kept my ground and remained in place. I wasn't afraid anymore. Somehow scaling that wall had given me something I didn't have before: I'd had an epiphany. This time I did not run. I faced the evil that had been chasing me for so long. He could no longer scare me—instead, I lunged straight at him! When I did, a supernatural strength infused and empowered me. I seized him by his shoulders. Then, like a rag doll I threw him up and over my head and into the cliff-edged abyss. I watched him fall helplessly, completely disappearing into the darkness. Then, in that moment, the storm disappeared, and the sun came out. This little girl and I stood there together, next to my car, on a level open road.

Then I woke up.

It would've been easy to chalk this whole thing up as one crazy dream, one that I should dismiss once the morning rays hit my pillow. But somehow, I knew doing that would've been like tossing out the lump of coal while missing the potential diamond. Indistinctively there was a sensing of the preciousness of it all. The details of this dream were incredibly clear, so distinct, they never left me. In fact, to this day, they never have. This dream forced me to stop and think about the fact that for most of my life I'd been running from many ominously threatening things "behind" me. And now, here I was, at the end of that road. I would never outrun any of them. I knew now, if I continued to stay in this place, fear would take everything, eventually swallowing me whole. I had to risk the vulnerability of opening a new door, though it meant stepping into the storm, into blind darkness. It had to be done, no matter what I might find looming there in the shadows of my mind.

With this same supernatural strength, His strength that came to me when I needed it most, my dream became a reality. I found not only could I stop running, but I also had a new ability to stand, face and eventually overcome so many of the chasing threats that haunted me. And she, the little one, who was there next to me every step of the way? The meaning was obvious.

She… was me. The me I had rejected long ago.

Over time, many of the puzzle pieces have slowly come into place, increasingly revealing the true picture. Through all the years, all the false labels I'd wrongly adopted, her true identity remained. Deep inside me, she was still there. Untouched. Unchanged. Unmarred. I've come to understand more about this person inside me. Though I'd rejected her, she'd never abandoned me. She was undaunted by my storms, unmoved by my fears, and remained true despite the lies that had piled high on top of her for years on end. She was and is my true God-given identity. She *is* me. I'd never lost her. She'd merely been buried. Silenced. Yet, all along my life's journey, she'd ridden there with me, next to me. She'd followed closely behind me through every twist and turn of this life. This young stranger was very intimately connected with me always–even if I never knew her at all.

It would take time. Time to unravel the answers, the mysteries of who she is. I'm still learning, of course. I think I always will be. Like any good relationship, the details and connections come slowly. It just so happens that He has all the time in the world to do the weaving between us. He alone is helping me discover all of who she is created to be.

God met me in my rejection.

# MY STORY

*Slowing Down to Pray & Reflect*

As I read Chapter Eight, I was reminded of my own…

When I think about what I just wrote, it makes me feel…

I think others see me as…

I see myself as…

The thing others have said about me that I've believed is…

The time rejection stung me the deepest was when…

The way I now avoid feeling that same rejection again is by…

I know I'm running from…

I let my emotions take the wheel when I…

The lie I have uncovered about myself is…

# PRAYERS & MEDITATIONS

## *Chapter 8*

But now, this is what the LORD says—he who created you, Jacob, he who formed you, Israel: "Do not fear, for I have redeemed you; I have summoned you by name; you are mine." Isaiah 43:1 (NIV)

For you created my innermost being; you knit me together in my mother's womb. I praise you because I am fearfully and wonderfully made; your works are wonderful, I know that full well. Psalm 139:13-14 (NIV)

Though my father and mother forsake me, the LORD will receive me. Psalm 27:10 (NIV)

The righteous cry out, and the LORD hears them; he delivers them from all their troubles. Psalm 34:17 (NIV)

For the LORD will not reject his people; he will never forsake his inheritance. Psalm 94:14 (NIV)

Where can I go from your Spirit? Where can I flee from your presence? If I go up to the heavens, you are there; if I make my bed in the depths, you are there. If I rise on the wings of the dawn, if I settle on the far side of the sea, even there your hand will guide me, your right hand will hold me fast. If I say, "Surely the darkness will hide me and the light become night around me," even the darkness will not be dark to you; the night will shine like the day, for darkness is as light to you. Psalm 139:7-12 (NIV)

…And surely I am with you always, to the very end of the age. Matthew 28:20 (NIV)

My Prayer…

# Chapter 9

# Meeting God in the Grocery Store

Setting down the syringe and snapping off his blue latex gloves, the surgeon turned to me with a serious look on his face. "Which hospital do you prefer? I recommend surgery to get this thing out as soon as possible."

"Wow! Okay? I wasn't expecting something like that so quickly. Can I ask why all the rush?" I responded, feeling blindsided.

"Because there appears to be blood in the sample I just drew. And blood usually means cancer. So, I recommend you get the surgery scheduled as soon as possible." His blunt response revealed his offense with my questioning. With that, he quickly stepped out of the room so I could change from my scratchy paper gown. Almost losing my balance while sliding on my jeans, I couldn't process his words just yet. Reality hit me on my way out the door, when the receptionist stopped me, "Here's some information to go over at home." She slid a small stack of pamphlets across the counter toward me. Obligingly I nodded and left with papers in hand. The drive home was surreal. I kept asking myself, *Did that just happen?*

Just a couple of weeks earlier, I'd found a small lump and scheduled an appointment with my regular doc to check it out. It was only a precaution. No big deal. Upon seeing me, my doctor had recommended further tests, just to be safe. He referred me to the physician I'd seen today. Now here I was, wham! Hit with the possibility of cancer? This whole thing was moving way too fast. It was too much.

Once I got home, I made a beeline straight to David. Ushering him into our bedroom, I quietly closed the door behind me. We didn't need the kids overhearing what I was about to share. The last thing I needed was for them to worry. "We need to talk." Concerned, he reached for the chair and sat down. I slowly lowered myself onto the edge of the bed, directly across from him. I opened my mouth, but no words would come. I wanted to explain what the doctor had just said, but instead could do nothing more than burst into tears.

In an effort to reset the moment, I jumped up and ran to our small bathroom. Yanking on the roll of toilet paper, I tore a small section and quickly wiped my wet eyes with it. I then returned to try again. With a deep sigh, I shared everything that had just happened at the doctor's office, then waited for some glimmer of wisdom to come from my man. He always knew just what to say to make me feel better. Leaning forward he grabbed my hand in both of his. Helping me try to break it all down into palatable pieces, he said, "Honey don't worry. Whatever it is, it's going to be okay. You don't even know it's cancer yet." He did his best to console me as again I wiped at the reoccurring flow of tears, this time using my sleeve.

"Ya, but the doctor today seemed pretty certain it was!" I argued my response. "He wants me to schedule surgery right away!!!" I wasn't ready to dismiss the fear that easily.

Feeling bad, David moved from the chair, and was now sitting hip to hip next to me on the bed's edge. He slid his arm protectively around my shoulder. "Babe, you're gonna be okay. Let's look at this for what it is. What's the very worst thing that can happen?"

"What's the worst thing that can happen? I could die! That's the worst thing that could happen!" I was shocked at his unexpected insensitivity. Seriously? Did he just make me say those words out loud?!

Undaunted, he continued his train of thought, "Yes, that may be true. You could die… But, look at it this way. You know God has you, right? Even if He were to take you home, would that be so awful? I mean the worst thing that could happen is that you would get to go to heaven and be with Jesus, right?" Again, this may have been his best attempt at encouraging me, but telling your anxiety-ridden wife her one-way ticket to see Jesus may have just been punched was a bad idea.

We'd been married for sixteen years. We'd not only raised the two girls, but had also been blessed with having two sons. Our family of six was my treasure and the thought of leaving them horrified me. With all this in mind, I responded, "I love God, but no. Absolutely not. I do NOT want to go to heaven right now. What I want is to be around to see our kids graduate and get married. I want to be here to know my grandkids. I want to grow old with you. I want the whole thing. I'm not ready to face any of this now." By this point I was sobbing and I didn't care where the tears went!

I know lots of women who receive news like this and take it with strength and dignity, leaning into their rock-solid faith. Me? Not so much. Not even close. I was a hot mess, I was freaking out. It wasn't because I didn't have enough faith. It was because, secretly, I was still stuck in it.

What I mean is, all these years since we'd gotten married, I had buried the guilt and fear about the divorce. Right about now, you're probably wondering how that could be, after reading an earlier chapter about God and the sunset proposal, huh? I wish I had an answer for you, but I don't. All I can say is that I *wanted* that experience to be true, but the reality was, I was having a difficult time taking it to heart completely. Even with a blatant miracle staring me in the face, all that theology pulsing through my veins couldn't easily be ignored, let alone, dismissed. I definitely believed that God had shown up for me, on the beach that late afternoon when David proposed. But still, there was another part of me that feared I'd wanted it so much that maybe it was all in my head. Now, with this cancer looming over my head, I had to come clean. I had to admit it. With all this faith I claimed to have and all that God had clearly done in my life, if that biopsy came back and said I had cancer, was I prepared to face death?

I wouldn't say no, but I couldn't say yes. I simply wasn't sure. My lingering fear of God's judgment had been exposed.

By my definition, I had been a fairly strong Christian for as long as I could remember. My faith in the existence of God or who Jesus is and all of that, never once wavered. None of that was my issue. My problem was with me and my failings. Repeatedly, I would still be surprised to find myself tied to my performance and how it directly translated to God's view of me. I silently had never let go of the fear that maybe He didn't really forgive me. Maybe I missed my chance to make things right with Him long ago. And now not only did He not love me, maybe this cancer was my punishment. This icy thought truly made me tremble inside. I may have been able to shove these feelings down for years, but now I knew I needed to find an answer. I couldn't put it off any longer. My life literally depended on it.

Upon the recommendation of Dave's cousin, I decided to wait on the surgery until I could get a second opinion with her doctor. This physician was a well-respected cancer specialist who was known for his compassion. I quickly scheduled the next available spot he had on the calendar. Unfortunately, it was a month out. It would be thirty days of sitting in this limbo between fear and faith. Heaven and hell. It was awful. The month was filled with emotion. I cried, I worried, and I prayed a lot. I tandemly begged God to forgive me in one breath, then to heal me in the next. The ceiling above my prayers seemed to be made of steel. The skies remained silent. It appeared to me that I was left on my own to figure it out. Like a kid being punished with a time out to sit and think about what they'd done wrong. I concluded this might be my fate.

Finally, the day came, and another biopsy was evaluated. The results came back quickly, and the office called wanting me to come back in. Sitting there on the exam table, I still remember the incredible kindness of my doctor. He took my face into both hands and looked me straight in the eyes to assure me of his wonderful news. The results were negative! I did NOT have cancer. It was so elating that it felt unreal. As cliché as it sounds, I was aware that I had just been handed a new lease on life.

Even with this perspective, and all the gratitude that sprang from it, I couldn't shake the shame I felt over the way I'd handled myself over the past few weeks. Where was my faith? I'd let my emotions run full throttle, with no restraint whatsoever. They dictated everything. In all the drama, my faith had all but disappeared. When I needed God most, I couldn't find Him. Even though I repeatedly prayed for His help, I really didn't think I was in a position to ask Him for anything. How had I managed this denial for so long? I couldn't believe how many years I'd buried this guilt, only to have it spew up stronger than ever when the crisis hit.

If I were looking for signs, He'd given me so many already. Why was it never enough? Why couldn't I cling to the certainty I'd been given? What was my problem? Why did I still worry that in the end, God would reject me? With these thoughts, I became determined: I would not let this guilt rule my life any longer. I would somehow go to the source and get the answer, once and for all.

It may sound silly, but I started with searching my Bible, for the millionth time, writing down every scripture I could find on the subject. Next, I went through every book in my home library, looking for any and all information I'd previously collected about Christians and divorce. The same thing began happening that had happened years before; all these activities were again only serving to confuse me more. But I kept at it, wading my way through the many opinions. Sorting out the mixed interpretations of what the Bible actually meant to say. I scoured bookstores for newly printed material, or those I may have missed in the past. Finally, I went to an option that I didn't have the first time: the internet. One website advised something that sounded like a magic trick. If I aimed these specific words toward heaven, poof! All my screw ups were guaranteed to disappear! That seemed easy and quite convenient. Another person had posted a surly article describing my sin and my fate in detail. His take was that I'd already committed an unforgivable sin. His take was simple: I was doomed. So many contradictions, once again. Each thing I read, whether in a book or online, all bent scripture toward whatever direction the writer desired. Whether it was grace, judgment, or self-saving, I could find it. It was all there. What did I want to see? So many loopholes were available if I wanted to use them. There was also a tremendous amount of hate if that's what I chose to see. The matter came down to this—either I was completely forgiven, or I was already damned. I would accept my fate, if only I could be sure of what it was. I didn't want loopholes to make me feel better. I wanted the truth. I knew how easy it was to twist scripture and make it say what I wanted it to say. I'd been sitting under those types of sermons for most of my life!

I felt like that lady in the Bible who tried to make her way through a crowd just to touch Jesus. There were so many people to get past, so much noise clamoring in her ears. So much shoving and pushing as everyone around her tried to claim a piece of God. I was this woman. I felt like I couldn't get near Him. There were so many voices swaying me this way and that. What did Jesus say to me? I clearly didn't know. I couldn't hear him above all they had to say. Every Pastor, church attender or internet site—all of them with their conflicting opinions. So much noise surrounding Jesus. Surrounding God. The false diagnosis of cancer had revealed that when it came right down to it, I stood with empty pockets when it came to my faith. Now I needed to press past that crowd, ignoring those voices. I had to get to the One and Only. He, alone, would tell me the truth. That is if He could even see me buried in that chaotic crowd. It was the chance I had to take. Even if I looked like a fool, I knew I had to try.

It was months of praying and asking Him to help me put this angst between us to rest. Whatever that meant. All I knew is that I wanted to be right with God. I wanted Jesus to call me His friend, not his regret. It was similar to the prayer I had prayed so many years ago before when David and I married. Here I was, over 15 years later, still praying the same prayer. How embarrassing. I was ridiculous. Yet, my prayers continued, "Lord, there is so much confusion surrounding You and what you want of me. Lord, I need to hear it from You alone. I won't accept anyone else's voice. I'll wait for yours."

One afternoon, I made a routine trip to the grocery store. It was a regular day, nothing at all special about it. Sliding my purse strap over my shoulder, keys in hand, I locked the car and headed in. Grabbing a shopping cart at the entrance, I wheeled inside. Right there at the front of the store, was a display. They were running a special. Cases of spring water were on sale. I stopped the cart to grab a couple. Because the cases are large and heavy, they're a bit awkward to put into the cart. I looked around me to make sure I wasn't blocking anyone. The area where I was standing was clear, not a soul near me. I heaved one twenty-four pack into the cart.

Quickly turning back, I grabbed a second, setting it on top of the first.

I then resumed my walk toward that first aisle. Pushing the cart forward, suddenly I stopped in my tracks. Now, you can judge me for what I'm about to say, surmise it however you like. But what I am about to share is exactly how it happened, it's the complete and unaltered truth (in the position my faith was in, I couldn't have made this up if I'd wanted to.) I stood there in the isle, frozen because I was immediately aware of a presence standing there in front of me. I didn't see Him, but I knew He was standing there in front of me, to the right. Now understand, I had not been thinking about God or Jesus or faith or anything of the kind when this happened. I was simply putting water into my cart and was on my way to get the next item on my grocery list. Nothing more.

It was at that moment, I heard the voice. It's hard to describe how I heard it, but I'll do my best. The voice came from outside of me, yet it was like a knowing inside of me. I'm sorry if that doesn't make much sense. It didn't come like voices normally do, yet I recognized it as such. It was softer, yet more penetrating. It was strong in authority. It was commanding yet kind. The words spoken were not exactly of an audible sense, yet somehow, they were. The best way I can describe it is that it was both a hearing and a knowing at the same time. What I can say is it was inarguably not of me. One simple sentence was all I heard, but it was more than I could have ever have imagined or asked for.

In that moment, this gentle voice spoke directly to me, *"Do you think your sin is bigger than my grace?"*

Ten words, so powerful, they changed everything in an instant. In that one unexplainable moment, sixteen long years of worry, shame, and guilt, fell forever to the ground. Without a doubt, I knew I had finally made my way through the crowd. Somehow, on an ordinary afternoon, in an ordinary place, I had touched *Him*.

Peace instantly and unmistakably filled my soul.

I met God in the grocery store.

# MY STORY

*Slowing Down to Pray & Reflect*

As I read Chapter Nine, I was reminded of my own…

When I think about what I just wrote, it makes me feel…

A time I was faced with my own mortality was when…

The way I handled the situation was by…

When I think about the afterlife - about eternity - it makes me…

My definition of God's grace…

When I consider my mistakes, I think grace is…

The lie I have uncovered about grace is…

# PRAYERS & MEDITATIONS

## *Chapter 9*

But he said to me, "My grace is sufficient for you, for my power is made perfect in weakness." 2 Corinthians 12:9 [NIV]

For it is by grace you have been saved, through faith—and this is not from yourselves, it is the gift of God. Ephesians 2:8-9 [NIV]

To the praise of his glorious grace, which he has freely given us in the One he loves. In him we have redemption through his blood, the forgiveness of sins, in accordance with the riches of God's grace. Ephesians 1:6-7 [NIV]

I sought the LORD, and he answered me; he delivered me from all my fears. Psalm 34:4 [NIV]

The righteous cry out, and the LORD hears them; he delivers them from all their troubles. Psalm 34:17 [NIV]

And God is able to bless you abundantly, so that in all things at all times, having all that you need, you will abound in every good work. 2 Corinthians 9:8 [NIV]

But he gives us more grace. That is why scripture says "God opposes the proud but shows favor to the humble." James 4:6 [NIV]

My Prayer…

# Chapter 10

# MEETING
# GOD IN MY CHOICES

*Y*ears ago, my car needed a specialty repair. The closest dealership able to do the job was located a few hours away, somewhere near our family cabin. We'd need to bring our vehicle in to their service department.

Since Dave had an impossible workload the week of our appointment, we both decided it made the most sense for me to make the lengthy but doable drive to the dealership alone. If I got up early, I could drop the car off, grab a rental and return home all in the same day. It wasn't a hard drive, just a long one. I wasn't worried about it. I'd been up that way on our family trips so many times before and knew it would be a piece of cake.

The small and seemingly unimportant caveat was, David had always been the one driving. I'd never stopped to think about the fact that in all those trips to the cabin together, I'd hardly noticed the blur of landscape routinely passing by my passenger window. My scattered ADD mind was all too often busily flipping through a catalog of distractions while he got us there. Reality was, I'd never *had to* pay attention to the actual route itself. I'd always just hopped in the passenger seat and buckled up—knowing in a few hours we'd arrive. But, with so many back-and-forth trips, surely I could manage getting to the dealership by myself. It was along the same route, just this time, I'd be the one driving. Doing it alone wouldn't make that much difference.

Back then, my vehicle (or phone) didn't have any type of navigation system. There was no option for that angelic all-knowing voice to effortlessly guide me along. In those days, the best I could hope for was to periodically glance at my crumpled paper of scribbled notes while keeping my car between the lines. Worst case, I could grab the multi-folded road map from my glove compartment, but it was much too big and would take way too long to use. This day I chose to simply rely on my keen sense of recall to get me where I needed to be. The drive was familiar. I didn't think twice about it.

About an hour into the morning, I spotted an upcoming merge of two highways. Automatically I thought I knew which way to go. *I'll stay right here in the left lane… Wait a second, what did that sign say? I missed it. Maybe I'm supposed to take the merge?*

A sudden panic rose in me as the realization hit—I had no idea which way to go! Why couldn't I remember where Dave went from here? I'd never really paid that much attention. Now I had to choose. These two roads would clearly take me in two different directions. The impending split was coming up quickly. My mind froze. At first, I'd thought I knew where I was going, but now at this moment, I'd lost all sense of direction. Nothing at all seemed familiar. Quickly scanning the panoramic view across my car windows, there wasn't a single thing that said, "Come this way…". No hint, no beckoning nod. Nothing. I took a deep breath. Then a second one. A strangely gentle thought suddenly broke in, interrupting my fear and settling me, *"Just stop where you are, Teri. Just pull over onto the shoulder and call Dave. He knows every inch of this area. He'll tell you which road to take."*

With this single thread of clarity, I hit the blinker and slowly made my way over, into the right lane, then off the pavement entirely. The car bumped and jolted as I rolled to a dusty stop on the rocky dirt, hoping I hadn't just added a flat tire to the mix. Quickly reaching for my cell phone, I pushed "Husband" in my contacts.

With a couple of rings, then a "Hey, honey!" instantly I could breathe again. All became right in a moment by simply hearing his voice.

After a few sentences, I learned the direction that I was tempted to go was *not* the right way. Had I chosen that route, I would have been going in the wrong direction. I would have wasted time, gas, perhaps gotten myself outside of cell range, and missed my appointment entirely! Now, with the confusion cleared, I made my way back onto the highway and eventually to my destination—with time to spare. I even managed to make it back home in the rental car before dark!

Looking back, what would that day have looked like, had I chosen to continue driving by my own sense of direction, instead of pulling off to ask? Sure, I had my gut feelings, but in this case, those would have led me in the wrong direction and quite possibly would have created an additional bucketload of problems as well. By simply stopping where I was, I got it right. I chose to stop and ask for direction—which helped me make it to my destination.

I made a wise choice that day.

I read someplace that the average adult makes approximately 35,000 choices per day. I was shocked to hear that. It's enough to make me want to pull the covers over my head and never leave my bed in the morning! But I bring it up to make this point. Even when we don't actively realize it, each of us exercises the power of choice thousands of times every single day. The good news about this is, even when I swear I'm stuck or unable to move from whatever circumstances have me bound, I am not powerless. I always have the ability to make a decision. We all do and we're doing it constantly. Big and small, right and wrong, good and bad, each of us are making our decisions every minute of every day. Even when we stall in our circumstances, fearing or simply refusing to make a choice, this action itself, is a choice made.

The beautiful yet terrifying thing about being human is our ability to affect (and sometimes *infect*) each other with what we choose to say and do. No man is an island, even if, sometimes, we wish we were. Ripple effects happen. Regardless of how I originally intended, there have been choices I've made that have inadvertently wounded others. It grieves me when I think about these actions of mine—whether in word or deed, how they've hit others and left lasting impressions. It rocks me to my core to think there are emotional dents or even scars left behind from something I did or said. It kills me. On the other hand, if what I've had to say, or something I've done inspired, comforted, or in any way made someone's load lighter, I'm elated. It makes me want to do more. Coming alongside someone and offering a healing salve to another's place of pain is an honor given. When I power through my days, focusing on my to-do list, I can be guilty of forgetting this most crucial fact.

I've rushed ahead, and sadly *missed it* many times. I miss the road when I'm too busy. I miss my turn when I don't take time to listen. When I don't stop to ask for direction, or don't seek to understand where the other person might be coming from, I miss it. I miss the road to deeper relationships, intimacy, and connection. I must slow down and sometimes even pull off the road completely. But when I shift it into park, I need to be careful. Sometimes when I'm sitting in one place, it's not to reflect, contemplate or to ask for clarity. On the contrary, I shut it down because I want to be left alone. When my feelings are hurt, or I'm angry, I can't see or hear anything but the blaring of my own emotions, I withdraw. I can't move forward when I can't see straight. Self-reflection and accountability are good, but I'll get nowhere if I choose to remain in my pain. I must be careful not to get stuck here. It's one thing to choose to stay in one place. It's quite another to feel unable to leave it. Inability to move equals imprisonment. That's what getting stuck feels like for me. Like a prison. There are times when I'm so very tired of the long road it feels like I can go no further. I must recognize the lie and move past it.

U-turns are an option at times. Even on the narrowest of roads, occasionally, a sign might pop up offering the opportunity to make right on a wrong decision. But, in those tight places, turning around is never easy. Though redemption might occur, and forgiveness granted, traveling back always comes at a relational cost. Not only is humility required to make that three-point turn, but there's also something much more fragile at stake. A tiny piece of the original innocence between us is ripped away and lost along the way back. A do-over is never quite the same as it could have been, had I or the other person taken the right road to begin with. This soberingly human truth is the somber reality that paralyzed me for years. It tries to stop me even now—if I let it.

It always comes down to a choice.

Certainly, the guilty regrets of negative experiences and the loss of precious time weren't the passengers I wanted sitting shotgun with me on the road of life. Their constant messages of shame distracted me from the road ahead. Even if I could've somehow ignored them, I wouldn't have. Why? Because often I'd find myself agreeing and even joining their conversation. I'd told myself that when it came right down to it, I lacked what it took to make good choices. I'd convinced myself that I had nothing good to offer anyone, that I'd brought others nothing but problems and pain. Looking over my shoulder at the road behind me, it felt like there was little if any positive value underneath this skin.

When this happened, I couldn't bear the realization that others thought less of me than I already thought of myself. Back then, I had no idea that most everyone struggles at one time or another with self-defeating internal messages. To me, I was strange, a loser. I was alone in this, unlike everyone else. I was the one who was hopelessly unable to make relationships work. My history proved it. I was nothing more than a weak and emotional weirdo who couldn't make a good decision if it killed me, and at the rate I was going, eventually, it would.

What scared me most? Instinctively, I knew that free will wasn't *free*. There'll always be a price tag attached. And I was racking up quite a bill. Mistakes are costly. Knowing this, paralyzed me at every fork in every relationship road. At a gut level, I knew soon enough, somewhere, sometime, somehow, I'd make a foolish decision, do or say something stupid and end up in a place I never wanted to be. And the saddest part of all? Often, I wouldn't even know when it was exactly that I'd make that destructive choice that would later find me on the outside looking in.

This type of thinking hedged closely to a victim mentality and one I'm not proud to admit I've had. I hated the way these resentful thoughts made me feel. Ignorant. Offended. Ashamed. Rejected. Yet I played the reel repeatedly. Mental anguish downpoured onto my bare head trickling its way into my heart. The memories came, one after the next, like a thunderstorm raining on a warped tin roof. And with each drop that hit, I'd repeatedly hurt all over again.

For me, despite the troubles in my life, I've longed to get past the pain and move forward—in a healthy way. It's just that many times, I couldn't. I simply didn't see a way, an avenue that led away from my negative cycles. Even if I thought to have caught the glimpse of a way out, I wouldn't know how to grasp it, or hold onto it long enough to create real change. I didn't know how to leave the toxicity. I'd been there so very long that roots had grown thick and woven under my feet. I despised this place and so many times tried to shake myself free, but sadly found myself desperately entwined with its chaos.

When the pain is scathing and the wounds run deep, to simply suggest embracing positive thoughts or to recite little prayers seems ridiculously absurd. To me, these were mockingly offensive gestures, and borderline cruel. Accepting a sing-song message of hope while I remained frozen in my pain, felt like a betrayal of self. Telling me to simply believe the best was like telling me to live blind or ignorant, or both. No, I couldn't allow myself to be that stupid again. Instead, I would often attempt to free myself by lashing out with everything in me. Taking this road was harsh, jagged and it often left bruises behind. These wounds were the worst of wounds, they were the permanent kind. Unseen with the eye, but with the heart that had twenty-twenty vision and could never forget what it saw. Relationships could be destroyed down this road.

Other than escalating already intense situations, knowing what didn't work offered me nothing. Keeping my mouth shut while nobly considering and accepting another's broken imperfections didn't do anything magical for me. Akin to offering a teaspoon of medicine to a dead man, it was pointless. It couldn't even come close to touching me in the darkness I'd fallen into. Sinking deep, depression would often wrap its dense cloak snugly around my shoulders. I'd cinch it in even tighter. I knew this road well; I'd memorized every groove carved into it. *Things will always be this way. You bring all of this upon yourself, so accept your fate. You will never change. You'll always wind up right here, alone.*

For years I swallowed these sewage messages like the sludgy garbage that they were. I believed I had no choice. I opened my mouth and fed myself the poison, *I am powerless.* It tasted bitter, yet

I swallowed it down. Like a stone, this lie sat heavy in my stomach. It didn't belong there yet seemed lodged permanently in place. How could it *not* be true? From where I sat, my own actions had slammed the iron door of this self-made prison. It was deadbolted, locked forever.

Sitting in this desolate place, despite myself, the impossible happened. It was in this bleak moment, in this jail cell of my own making, that it came. The seemingly tiny, fragile sprout of a *new decision* pushed its way through the cold and unforgiving concrete that surrounded me. It could be my hand that chose to pluck it up and crushed it in my drawn fist. Or, I could get down on my knees and lean in toward it. I could consider it. I could nurture it. I could follow its leading. I witnessed firsthand how even in the most impossible of spaces and times, the gift of hope indeed springs eternal.

What I do when the gift appears is always up to me.

As I have mentioned in many chapters in this book it's in these moments—when I've felt alone, filled with anxiety, powerless to go on—that thankfully the light has come. When do I see it? When I stop absentmindedly running ahead. When I stop insisting on going my own way, it appears. I don't see it when I'm certain I have all the answers. No, never. It comes when I'm more than aware that I have none. When I arrogantly assume which road is best, I will invariably miss it. But, when I'm keenly aware of my own vulnerability—the high likelihood that I can get lost easily—that's when it faithfully comes shining into my darkness, leading the way.

When I've made my bed at what I'm certain is the deadest of dead ends, life can still spring forth out of nowhere.

Even though lies can feel so very true, and chokingly dictating at times, they never belong in the driver seat. Nor do they have the power to hold me in one place. The truth is, NOTHING can keep me captive, if I don't allow it to. With His help, I can move in the right direction. I don't just say this, off-the-cuff. He has proven this truth to me. He alone shatters the lies when they come for me, reminding me I am more than the chaos that surrounds me, more than the foolish choices that I make. He reminds me that He is committed to the process and will never abandon me in it. I'm not alone and stranded on the side of life's road, even when I feel certain that I am. Now I can see the lie for what it is. I don't have to listen to its condemning voice that says I'll always be rejected, that I have no value to anyone. I know now, the lie speaks its native tongue, not mine.

Making choices doesn't have to paralyze me. No longer does it come with the dread of making a mistake that will hurt me or someone else because it isn't about relying on my own reasoning or clever ideas to get me from A to B. If it were, I'd still be back there, crashed in some ditch. It's about stopping to ask and trusting the whisper of His leading. Maybe all this spiritual GPS stuff seems silly to some, as it did to me at one point in my life. But I've changed my tune after landing in that ditch too many times. I know I can't afford to move an inch without it.

I have been given free will, *choice*, for a reason. It's a gift and an invitation. I'm free to use it any way I choose and so are you. To go my own way, and ignore that inner small voice is always an option, sure, and I still make that foolish decision sometimes. Yet, He still proves faithful to answer even when I call Him from there. And yes, I still make my share of U-turns, and see Him bring lessons from my mistakes. But now, I'm more aware and try to remember how very costly these lessons are as well.

When I choose to purposefully quiet the chatter around me, I will be able to hear the gentle whisper when it comes…. *"Just stop where you are, Teri. Just pull over onto the shoulder and call. He knows every inch of this area. He'll tell you which road to take."*

Moment by moment, I meet God in my choices.

# MY STORY

*Slowing Down to Pray & Reflect*

As I read Chapter Ten, I was reminded of my own…

When I think about what I just wrote, it makes me feel…

The times I tend to rush ahead are…

An example of a time I followed my impulses…

Later, the outcome was…

If I follow my emotions, they tend to lead me…

Stopping to pray before making decisions feels…

A time I've gotten stuck, unable to move forward…

The reason I felt stuck there was because…

I do / don't believe God cares or expects me to include Him in my choices.

The lie I have uncovered about my choices is…

# PRAYERS & MEDITATIONS

## *Chapter 10*

Seek his will in all you do, and he will show you which path to take. Proverbs 3:6 (NLT)

You make known to me the path of life, you will fill me with joy in your presence, with eternal pleasures at your right hand. Psalm 16:11 (NIV)

You who fear him, trust in the LORD—he is their help and shield. Psalm 115:11 (NIV)

Do not conform to the pattern of this world, but be transformed by the renewing of your mind. Then you will be able to test and approve what God's will is—his good, pleasing and perfect will. Romans 12:2 (NIV)

Here I am! I stand at the door and knock. If anyone hears my voice and opens the door, I will come in and eat with that person, and they with me. Revelation 3:20 (NIV)

In their hearts humans plan their course, but the LORD establishes their steps. Proverbs 16:9 (NIV)

Seek the LORD while he may be found, call on him while he is near. Isaiah 55:6 (NIV)

The righteous person may have many troubles, but the LORD delivers him from them all. Psalm 34:19-20 (NIV)

My Prayer…

# Chapter 11

# MEETING GOD
# IN MY WORDS

*T*here was no way I could relax enough to fall asleep. I couldn't stop thinking about all the awful things that had come out of my mouth earlier. Sure, I was angry, but did I really have to blast him like that? I was ashamed of myself. It was a colossal argument—one of our worst ever. During it, I'd said some pretty hurtful things to my husband. Now, I was feeling the remorse.

He'd done something that he knew I wouldn't like. When I found out about it, I was furious, as he'd expected I would be. That made matters worse. With my hot head ready to explode, I dumped all reasoning overboard leaving the helm wide open for my mouth to take over. Once that happened, there was no going back. Every ounce of my hostility was aimed dead center, rapid-speed firing at my man. I was showing no mercy. It only took a few minutes for me to thoroughly express my feelings on the matter. With deliberate, heart-slicing descriptives, my intent was to split him wide open for what he'd done. He'd hurt me, and now I was dead set on making sure he tasted his share of that pain. It was war, and when it came to verbal attacks, I was a much better sniper!

When the argument ended, I stood there with my arms folded tightly to my chest, still glaring him down. The room was now deadly silent. Emptied of verbal ammo, a smug satisfaction came over me as I viewed the carnage. He sat there, slumped forward, his elbows hinging on the edges of his knees. His chin was as low as it possibly could be. Judging from his position, I'd clearly won this round. My thoughts in that moment held nothing more than an indignant hope that maybe this time I'd gotten through to him. I felt strong. Self-vindicated. If he wasn't going to give me my validation in the moment, I was determined to at least be heard!

My justification for my behavior? Everything I'd just said (more like yelled), was nothing but the "truth." In my mind, that made it okay.

The truth isn't always *pretty,* and it wasn't my fault if he couldn't handle it. He should have thought about that long before he made the choice that started the fight to begin with. I'd only spoken the obvious. I was merely defending myself. He owed me an apology. At least that's how I saw it. Shrugging my shoulders at my own behavior, I was unmoved by his wounded expression… until now, hours later.

Time after time, whatever emotion had me in its grip, I felt the need to express it at full force. Whether it was fear, anger, or disappointment with Dave—or anyone I was close to—this was my standard practice of communicating when I felt disrespected. Shooting off my mouth was a regular way of life for me, even if I regretted much of what I said afterwards. And I always did. But in those moments, I was under the illusion that I was just *being honest.* And since honesty is what I valued most, I thought the blaring of naked truth made me authentic.

I couldn't see that my honesty made me nothing more than a royal jerk! And sadly, I was a very honest person. Everyone around me had the scars to prove it!

We all know the nursery rhyme about "sticks and stones," I think it's a terrible mantra to teach a kid! Broken bones may hurt, but at least they eventually heal—usually growing back stronger than before. Wounding words on the other hand can stab so deeply, their jagged echoes continue for years. In some cases, they can last a lifetime.

I remember years ago, my mom telling me, "Teri, not everyone wants to hear your version of the truth!" I had absolutely no idea what she meant by that. Back then, there was no way she could have explained it if she'd tried. Though I didn't understand, I never forgot what she said. It would be several years and a lot of pain, before I finally made the connection. Until then, I'd often return to ponder her phrase, wondering why people wouldn't want my honesty. It made no sense. Did others prefer I refrain from telling them the truth? How odd a thought. Why would anyone deliberately want to be fed lies? Is that how life and relationships were supposed to work? Surely that couldn't be what mom meant.

It wasn't a secret that my communication style—my paper-thin filter—had something to do with my difficulty making friends (or keeping them). Don't get me wrong, I had friends growing up (God bless them). I just wasn't good at it. Since it had been this way most of my life, I'd come to the conclusion that when it came to other women, things were just going to be hard. Even as an adult, attending an event where there'd be a large group of ladies, I'd show up with a knot in my stomach, if I showed up at all.

For me, it's often felt like standing behind a plate glass wall, with everyone else on the other side. I was there in plain view. So were they. All of us in the same place, just not "together." The feeling of isolation became my norm. From the other side, I could see their conversations, their laughter, their generous hugs. I watched it all from my side of the glass, from where I stood… alone.

Spotting women who'd mastered the art of connection was easy; just look for the tribe. Leading it, there'd always be an irresistible magnet to which others couldn't help but be drawn. These were the chosen ones. The lovely ones. The admired ones. The social butterflies that fluttered around the room. Many were thrilled when she'd land near them. Those butterflies never came past the glass. I never was a butterfly.

In my obvious insecurity, I was more like the cactus in the room. No one wants to hang out near a cactus.

Cactuses may bloom a bright flower which catches an eye for a moment. But no one comes too close to a cactus, even one with a flower. And forget about a hug. Considering how often it happened, I was forced to conclude that I must be a stickery person—at least on the outside. I felt misunderstood. This made me resentful. Often, I wanted to yell from my side of the glass, "Hey! Come on! I'm not that prickly!" But from where I stood, no one could have heard me anyway.

At work it wasn't much different. I'll admit, client relationships were easier by far than the personal ones. With paying clients, I knew what was expected between us—so did they. They paid for my time, and I delivered professional service. It was cut and dry. No guesswork. New clients would come while others moved on. I never took any of it personally. Business was business. It was the people I worked alongside each day that created my angst. That was personal. Since most of my coworkers were female, as usual I felt like the odd woman out. I genuinely liked many of these ladies, but once again, from their coolness, the feelings didn't appear mutual. Often, I would walk into the crowded breakroom and suddenly the buzzing would go quiet, only to pick up again once I stepped away. I found it strange. The times they did keep up the chatting or laughter, it would have something to do with some inside joke or recent outing they'd shared outside of work. It didn't feel great never being included, but I tried to shake it off and dismiss the obvious. Each day I'd come in, do my job, and go home to my family, without the invite, without the friendly bantering, without the friendships.

I worked this way for over a year, until one day I took a chance. I lamented to a coworker about my paranoia of being disliked, hoping she would dismiss my fears. Instead, she didn't hesitate to fill me in, telling me it wasn't my imagination. She had no problem sharing that I truly was less than a favorite around there! OUCH! Apparently, the others felt I was too closed off. They saw me as someone who was merely there for my clients then rushed home to my family. To them, I appeared self-focused. My face burned with embarrassment at the thought of how they saw me. I instantly wanted to defend myself saying, *No! That's the opposite of how I feel! I've always wanted to be included!* But I couldn't really say that because the truth was, she was technically right. I never stayed after hours just to hang out. (But why would I, with the way they treated me?) I was a mom of four and also managed all my husband's office work for his company. My spare time was extremely limited. But no one seemed to take that into account. And as far as preferring to chat with my clients more than with coworkers, of course I did! I called that great customer service! How had carrying out my responsibilities gotten translated into me being unfriendly and unapproachable? Why was this label once again being pinned on me? I winced at the recurring pinprick.

It was as if I'd traveled back in time to sixth grade. Once again, I was that awkward schoolgirl standing alone, just waiting to be chosen—yet was always the last to be picked for the team. But this wasn't a playground game, and I was no longer a child. I didn't understand when it happened as a kid, and I certainly didn't understand it now. I was loyal and honest. So why did others turn away? What was the problem with *me*?

I spoke what I felt and for some reason that was the wrong thing to do. Once again, the message confused me. Was I supposed to lie in order to be accepted? I hated being lied to. I avoided liars at all costs. Those who fabricated stories had no place in my life. Swallowing something only to find out later it was untrue, made me feel gullible.

Foolish. I had no time for that. What's the point in talking if what you're saying has no substance? It's disrespectful and an incredible waste of everyone's time. Early in my life, I'd vowed to never be that person. Why did it now seem that honesty was taboo?

Each of us has a specific way we see things, how we interpret others and the world around us. It's our point of view, our perspectives that make us human. But what happens when my point of view casts a shadow over yours? Is that right or fair? What do we do with our versions of the truth? How can I remain true, without projecting my beliefs, my take, onto someone else's conflicting view? And how do I keep from falling into the easier trap of simply telling others what they want to hear in an effort to keep the peace?

When we don't agree, does that have to mean one of us is wrong?

Who determines what is right? What is true?

Through my loneliness, I learned a painful lesson firsthand; that my words and actions are incredibly powerful. They can wound and they can heal. And when we don't agree, or when I'm faced with a threatening situation, how I choose to speak or act in those moments has a lot to do with what happens next. Though I'm a slow learner in this area, I think most people understand this concept. Collectively, we may understand it, but the question is will we remember to practice it when the heat turns up to a high flame? Like the rudder that turns the ship, my words and actions dictate much of what I will eventually see and feel manifesting in my life. So many times, I've spoken fear, panic, and dread, only to see the isolation it brings afterwards. Without knowing it, I was unwittingly inviting these negative emotions to grow in prominence into my reality.

Once I became aware of this destructive pattern, I was eager to change. I prayed for His strength to help me put this new awareness into practice. On my own, it was too easy to default back into my old patterns. It would have to be Him in me, if there would be any hope of real change. I knew that now and it wouldn't be long before I was given an opportunity to walk it out:

During a routine exam, my doctor noticed a small, yet strange-looking area on my back and asked me to tell him more about it. Since it was an old scar left there from my twenties, I quickly dismissed his concern explaining how it was nothing. He didn't seem to feel the same way about it and asked if he could do a biopsy right then. I agreed, even though I was sure it was a waste of his time. In just a few days, I had a voicemail to call him back and to ask for the doctor himself. I did. His voice had a serious tone, which I'd never heard from him before. The results of the biopsy weren't good. I had a very rare type of cancer in my back, and it needed to come out immediately. He went on to say he'd only seen two cases like it in his entire career. He'd instructed his office to go ahead and schedule my surgery with a local surgeon who specialized in this type of cancer removal. Judging from the high numbers on the lab results, the cancer needed to be removed immediately. I was being placed at the top of the list. He told me not to delay or put this off in any way, "When the surgeon calls with your appointment, take it. Don't dismiss this. Get this thing out as soon as possible."

You will recall my story from years before, when I didn't have cancer, but thought I did—and how I'd handled that news. This time, it was really happening, and this time, I chose to do it differently. I would choose my words and my behavior instead of letting my fear dictate them for me. In the throes of this life-threatening news, it would be apparent to all if I was changing for the better, or if it was all talk. I let Dave know what the doctor had said. But this time, I gave him the news with a positive view. I told him I had cancer, but in the very next breath, I quickly pointed out how grateful I was that it was found! Especially considering how I'd tried to discount and discourage the doctor from thinking twice about it that day. Delivering this hard message to him in this way also helped him remain hopeful about my outcome. With the absence of the crying or hysteria, as I had displayed years before, we both were able to stay focused on the good, seeing the light at the end of this dark tunnel.

After we spoke, I didn't run to google and check the cancer stats. Instead, I deliberately refused to think on it at all. I simply went back to what I'd been doing before receiving the call that day. In that moment, I had to choose: I would either dwell in the fear or I would give this whole thing to God in a prayer. Consciously deciding I would not spend a moment in the negative, I refused to allow fear to sneak in through the back door. I purposely set my mind on all the GOOD things in my life. Instead of the worry, I filled my mind with all the blessings that God had been so good to give to me. I chose to express my gratitude for each of them, instead of naming the list of *what ifs*. Even the cancer diagnosis itself became a source of gratitude. It turned from a threatening death sentence to a thankful prayer. I focused on the fact that God had stirred the doctor's heart to check a spot that had been there for decades. A spot that I had tried to convince him to dismiss.

Dave was scheduled to leave the country on a mission trip with some friends from our church to help others who needed their skills. I would most likely face this surgery alone, as I was unwilling to have Dave cancel his trip. I knew I would be okay. This time I would live what I said and believed, knowing I was in God's hands, not my husband's. The surgeon's office called that same day with my surgery date. They had placed me with the earliest morning appointment at the beginning of their day—the following Friday. It was one day before Dave left for the trip! He would be there after all. Again, I thanked God for these immediate blessings. Months before all of this, I had scheduled a family tea party for the ladies in our family. It was supposed to be held that upcoming Saturday, the day after my surgery as well. Many of my family members had told me how much they were looking forward to the fun get-together. I decided, once again, I would walk this out in faith. I would not cancel the party.

Friday came bright and early. I remained calm, keeping my thoughts corralled in a positive frame. While sitting there in the main waiting room, each time I felt twinges of fear trying to creep in, I'd immediately send them packing. Finally, they called my name, and with that I kissed Dave and headed back. Soon the surgery was underway. Almost eight hours and over one hundred stitches later. The orange-sized cancer was entirely removed. They got it all!

I now have a scar, a red line that runs horizontally across my back. From my spine to my waist, I carry with me a permanent reminder that I'm blessed to be alive. This is what I allow to remain from what I have been through. A gift of remembrance that encourages me. It encourages others as well. I could share my story in a way that makes me look "brave." But that would put the focus on me—and that would be a lie. God was the real hero of my cancer story. His love is what held me steady through the whole ordeal. His love was the compass that directed my thoughts, my words and my actions throughout that whole ordeal.

Before I speak, I now try to stop and ask myself, *What's my motive? Am I trying to elevate myself or am I coming from a place of love?* Love needs to be the place I start. But it's not the only thing I must do. Many times I've said something from a place of love, yet still found myself inadvertently hurting another. When this happens, what might be missing?

I've learned not only must my words come from a place of love, but I must also not forget to "wrap my words" in love. In the past, Dave would often say to me, "It's not *what* you said to me, Teri. It's *how* you said it!" If I speak truth without love, the words come across harsh and uncaring. The hearer rejects them out of a natural self-protection. Blunt truth is useless at best, and wounding at worst. Of course, sometimes authentic truth does indeed "hurt.' But it's the good kind of hurt, like the washing of a scrape to get the dirt out. The motive is to remove what's harmful to make way for healing. Without the painful, but necessary attention to the toxic, restoration can never have its full growth in us. Real love NEVER seeks to harm. It only seeks to heal. That's why speaking truth must not only come from a *place* of love, but it must also be *wrapped* in it. And now, when I know what I'm about to say will be especially hard to hear, I try to remember to *double wrap it!!!*

I'm still far from perfect at it, but I do my best to refuse biting the bait of judging others then commenting thereupon. It's still tempting at times, but I know the lure always comes with that hidden deadly hook of hurting others. I remind myself to leave the assignment of motive to the only One who really knows. Only God can see their true heart. I never will. He knows the truth behind every action. I don't. He not only knows the truth, He *is* the Truth. This world and everything in and beyond it came into existence through His words. He created everything we know and see by simply speaking it to be so. I am here because He spoke. My very life helps me understand how powerful words are. My responsibility is to choose mine carefully.

I am so very grateful God met me in my words.

# MY STORY

*Slowing Down to Pray & Reflect*

As I read Chapter Eleven, I was reminded of my own…

When I think about what I just wrote, it makes me feel…

In regards to using my verbal filter, my words often sound…

The thing I most regret saying is…

At the time, my justification for saying it was…

Something I could have done differently would have been to…

When it comes to being honest, I am…

When speaking the truth, I do / don't care how my words will affect the other person.

If I could see inside others' hearts, I would / would not find many unnecessary wounds from my words.

I have often / rarely / never considered love to be the baseline for my actions and words.

The lie I have uncovered about my words is…

# PRAYERS & MEDITATIONS

## *Chapter 11*

Instead, speaking the truth in love, we will grow to become in every respect the mature body of him who is the head, that is Christ. Ephesians 4:15 (NIV)

Finally, brothers and sisters, whatever is true, whatever is noble, whatever is right, whatever is pure, whatever is lovely, whatever is admirable—if anything is excellent or praiseworthy—think about such things. Philippians 4:8 (NIV)

But the things that come out of a person's mouth come from the heart, and these defile them. Matthew 15:18 (NIV)

Pleasant words are a honeycomb, sweet to the soul and health to the bones. Proverbs 16:24 (NIV)

It is foolish to belittle one's neighbor, a sensible person keeps quiet. Proverbs 11:12 (NIV)

A gentle answer quiets anger, but a harsh one stirs it up. Proverbs 15:1 (GNT)

May the words of my mouth and the meditations of my heart be pleasing to you, O LORD, my rock and my redeemer. Psalm 19:14 (NLT)

Blessed are the merciful, for they will be shown mercy. Matthew 5:7 (NIV)

The words of the reckless pierce like swords, but the tongue of the wise brings healing. Proverbs 12:18 (NIV)

Those who are kind benefit themselves, but the cruel bring ruin on themselves. Proverbs 11:17 (NIV)

My Prayer...

# Chapter 12

# MEETING GOD IN MY MAMA

*M*ost little girls grow up having a close connection with their mama. I was no exception. As a young child, I adored my mom and was practically fastened to her at the hip. I'm not sure if she loved it or if it drove her a little crazy—maybe it was a little of both? But she was my mom and there was nowhere else on earth my young self wanted to be other than next to her… wherever that was.

Mom was sassy. A contrary paradox, she was a mixture of coy shyness and fiery temper. She was a short, round powder keg with a long but feisty fuse. Heaven help us all when that fuse got lit. If it did, you knew to run for cover, quick!

My mom was far from perfect. She definitely was no saint. I'd never want to paint her in that kind of light. Because to do that, I'd be erasing a lot of what made her, *Sylvia*. The truth is she was lovely… a lovely mess. And that mess was certainly loved by many. As a little girl, I stood at the front of that line.

She would often share stories of the tornadoes and thunderstorms that used to frighten her while growing up in the south. It made me glad to be born in California. Even as a grown woman and mother of three, when a thunderstorm came clapping over our house, she became a child once more, still terrified by those storms. At any given time, the worst of her fears would come rushing to the surface. I'm not proud to say, I had little tolerance for it back then. I often resented her for those childish ways. I'd felt cast as the adult she was supposed to have been. But, somewhere along the line, over the years, I too picked up many of those irrational fears, claiming them as my own.

For all the ways we differed, fear made us very much alike.

As we talked about in a previous chapter, I often struggled with thoughts that God was far from me and how I often spoke to mom about it. She was transparent with her stories of seasons in her own life when she too felt that God had left her side. She told me how in her panic, she would call her dad, my grandpa. She'd be in tears just needing to talk. With him there on the other end of the line, her worries about sins and forgiveness tumbled out of her heart and into his listening ear. She said he always took time to talk her off the ledge, reminding her that God's love and grace were always there for her; that she hadn't gone too far. He'd remind her of God's promises and that if she held onto them, she would make her way through whatever had her troubled. Her stories always filled me with hope, just like her dad's stories did for her.

In a season when I was struggling the most, mom got creative in her prayers for me. She hated to see me in such confusion regarding my faith, so she did what she always did: She got on her knees. This time though, she was asking a detailed request of the Almighty. At the time I had no clue of this.

It was early summer as I stood in the kitchen, putting food together. We were planning a picnic that day with our three kids. Zach, who was a little over two at the time, came running into the kitchen. Stopping to scoop him up, I squeezed a hug then sat him on the counter next to me and then turned my attention back to packing. While sitting there, something caught my son's eye. Quietly, he'd reached over toward a small ceramic container, pulling out a little red card. This container was very special to me. It was shaped like a tiny loaf of bread with a rectangle hole in the top that held a collection of small cardboard cards with scripture verses printed on each one. Each card still held its color, though all were faded from time, still I treasured this little thing. It was my mother's and used to sit on our kitchen counter when I was a kid. Because I loved it so much, eventually, when I grew up, she gave it to me. Ever since then it has had a permanent place in my kitchen. That day it sat on the counter next to my inquisitive little boy.

I hadn't noticed his tiny hand holding the scripture card up to his face pretending to read it, until I heard his sweet little voice say, "Babbeeebabbeebabbeeeeey."

Startled, yet smiling at the sweetness of the moment, I commented, "Honey, are you reading a scripture?"

He nodded, repeating his phrase. "Babbeeebabbeebabbeeeeey."

Since he kept saying the same thing, I bent one ear a little closer in an attempt to identify this mystery word, "Are you saying BABY?"

He grinned, bobbing his head up and down, happy that I had deciphered his gibberish. I couldn't help but engage him further, "Where is the baby?"

Again, his cherub cheeks plumped with pride as he repeated himself once more, "Baby!"

Having this playful discussion with my two-year old, while mentally checking off the items still needed for our trip, I half-mindedly asked my tot, "Is someone having a baby?" This time he sat up tall with the biggest gleeful expression as he yelled, "Yes!!!"

At this point I stopped packing. I turned and stared my little man square in the face. He had my full attention now. The funny banter was taking an interesting turn. I said, "Oh really?" I was intrigued at where my young son was taking this conversation, "Who's having a baby, Zach?"

Tracking with me completely, he didn't miss a beat. Without hesitation, he pointed directly at me and confidently replied, "You are!"

At that, I laughed out loud. What a creative little scenario he'd just entertained me with. It was clever and too cute. But then, as the minutes passed, something started to sink in. This past week I'd been feeling off. I'd been wondering if I was coming down with some kind of virus or something. Now, with my young son's assertive statement, I found myself adding up calendar days in my head! Was it possible? Reaching my hands underneath his tiny arms, I slid him down from the countertop. His bare little footsteps pattered behind mine as I made my way through the laundry room and swung open the door to the garage where David was. "Stay here with daddy while mommy runs to the store really quick," I told my little guy as I motioned to Dave that he was now on kid duty without any explanation of why. As crazy as it sounded, I just had to know if there was any chance that what my son had just announced could be true.

Grabbing the keys, I tossed out a quick, "Be right back," as I jumped in the car. Waving through the window of the driver's seat, to my bewildered husband who was standing there with a toddler pinned to his leg, I quickly backed out the driveway and was gone. I had to get my hands on a pregnancy test kit pronto! One item was all I needed. In and out of that store, I was back home in minutes. I headed straight for the bathroom with my little white box. While waiting for the line to appear or not, my mind raced. Had I recently said anything in front of Zachary about a baby? I didn't think so. There was nothing that I could recall. Being pregnant was the farthest thing from my mind that month. Life had been busy and honestly, until about thirty minutes ago, having a baby was the last thing I was thinking about. *So where did this kid get this idea?*

*Where was this coming from?* My swirling thoughts were interrupted by the faintest blue line beginning to appear right before my eyes. I AM PREGNANT! No way! But YES way! There it was in blue and white, undeniable. This was unreal. I was going to have a baby just like Zach had said. It was true! The little guy was spot on. I stumbled into the garage to tell his father the news. With the dual-lined strip still dangling from my limp hand, we both stood there completely stunned.

The next week I followed up with my doctor for confirmation. He concurred with the home pregnancy test results. I was indeed pregnant. He then calculated how far along I might be, then assigned me the official due date—March 12th. My mother's birthday.

I decided it would be fun to wrap up the original test wand and give it to my mom as a gift. I stopped by the hair salon when she was in between clients and had a few minutes. Walking up to her, I held out the wrapped box with her name on it, "Here's an early birthday gift, mom. This is a small part of the larger gift on order. The rest of your gift won't be ready until your actual birthday."

A look of cheerful bewilderment crossed her face knowing her birthday was several months away. What could this be? She reached out her open hand for the wrapped "gift" and gently pulled on the strand of the ribbon which held the box in place. Carefully lifting the small lid, the truth-telling plastic wand was revealed. She shot a look up from the box, wide eyed, "What *is* this?"

Smiling a quirky smile, I said, "It's a positive pregnancy test for your next grandchild that's due on your birthday next year!!!"

For a moment, joy exploded across her face, then suddenly she gasped, "YOU DON'T KNOW WHAT I PRAYED!"

Far from the response I'd expected, I replied, "Whaaat? What do you mean?"

"You don't know what I prayed!" She repeated as she stood there staring at the opened "gift" in her hand. "I know that God Himself is the author of life so I prayed and asked Him if He would give you a baby to show you He still cares for you and that He has not left you. This baby is a gift!"

Standing there stunned I had no response for this. Hearing that my mother had been secretly asking the Creator of life to "give me a baby to let me know he loves me" was kind of sweet but kind of crazy. Then to try to absorb the fact He'd clearly heard and answered that prayer was blowing my mind. She said, "I didn't tell anyone I was praying that prayer! It was between me and the Lord." *Wow. Hey mom, you think you might have wanted to clue me in when you're gonna pray prayers that involve me having a baby?* I had no idea what to do with all this information other than to simply hug her.

Mom was indeed a prayer warrior. I knew this all my life. It wasn't until many years into my adulthood that I realized her childlike ways were exactly the reason her faith was so strong. My resentment slowly transformed to an admiration for the simplicity she carried— especially when it came to things of God. When she felt powerless or fearful, prayer was always her go-to arsenal. When life was more than she could manage, God was her main source of comfort. She always went straight to Him. Many times, I'd walk into the house and find her face down on the living room carpet, arms extended, just crying out for His help. I know those very prayers protected me and my brothers from many avoided mishaps and dangers that we otherwise would have faced.

As far back as I can recall, this faith was always planted deep within her. It was forever there. And though most of her life she struggled with fear, I'm proud to say I was there as a witness when that very fear left her and her faith exploded in ways I would never have predicted. It was at the unlikeliest of times, when any one of us might succumb to the worst of our fears. It was when she heard the doctor say, "Stage four cancer. It's terminal."

I remember the day I found out. She had called with the news, and I dropped everything and immediately drove to my parent's home. She greeted me at the door with a faint smile that contrasted with her puffy red eyes.

"I'm glad you're here," she greeted me with a hug as we went into the family room where my dad was sitting with her. "The Lord and I have already had a good talk about this," she proceeded to share. "I told Him, 'Lord I'm praying that you heal me from this cancer as I know You can. But even if You don't, it will be okay. Whether You choose to heal me, or take me home, let this be used for Your glory.'" After hearing her say that, I respectfully replied, "Well, that is an amazing prayer, mom." Her faith reached in and pulled mine to the surface. I, too, knew it would be okay, no matter what came.

The oncologist who was overseeing mom's care met with us in the hallway after her initial exam. After reviewing the test results and the examination, we were given the grim news. According to the doctor's best estimation, mom had approximately six months before the cancer would take her from us.

But mom didn't let the news affect her attitude. She didn't show one ounce of fear. Her mood remained unbelievably jovial. Throughout the entire chemotherapy process, that woman amazed me. This made her oncologist uncomfortable on one hand yet intrigued on the other. She kept asking mom, "You realize your diagnosis, right? You're not going to survive this." Mom would just smile, nod and reply, "I understand." I witnessed this personally. The doctor was almost frustrated that my mom wasn't showing normal emotions of a terminal patient. Instead, she sat there peacefully swinging her short little legs back and forth under the edge of the exam table. Who does that? She wasn't in denial. She knew something the doctor didn't know. She knew she had a Heavenly Father who was right there with us in that room. She knew her God was so much bigger than this cancer could ever be. And He, not the lab results, would determine her days. She would continue telling her little jokes to every nurse, attending doctor, or medical personnel who happened to be near enough to hear them. There was absolutely no fear. Because of this, she quickly became a nurse favorite in the chemo department. One or two of them became so attached that they called her by her southern nickname, *Sylvie-June.*

A couple of months into her first round of chemo treatments, she was feeling particularly ill. We took her to the emergency room. The hospital ended up admitting her and giving her an IV of fluids. Mom had always been fearful of hospitals. Having rarely ever been admitted, other than having her kids and one surgery during her lifetime, she was not a fan. I was concerned how this stay would affect her emotionally.

Once admitted, I was there in the hospital room, trying my best to comfort and encourage her. With a childlike confession, she admitted she was very frightened. It was the first time I'd seen this fear show up again. But the reason wasn't what I thought it would be. She wasn't scared about her illness. She was fearful of being in a hospital bed and being left there all alone. As I held her hand, I reminded her that God never leaves us. It was the same reminder that she'd given me so many times in my life. I hated to leave her that evening but had to. There was a Christmas dinner that had previously been scheduled some time before all this. It was with some of Dave's extended family, and I was expected to be there. Before walking out the door of her room that evening, I left her with a hug, a kiss, and a promise. I'd be back first thing the next morning.

Making good on my word, I was up early, dressed and on my way down to the hospital. It was about a half hour from my house. Slipping into her room, I glanced at the bold numbered clock hanging there on the wall. It was just a little after 7:00 am when I arrived. Good! She probably would be sleeping. I slowly peeked around the half-pulled curtain to gently say good morning. Her bed was empty! My heart stopped for a moment. "Mom???" I called out, trying not to panic.

A faint reply came from behind the bathroom door, "Ya?" I sighed a huge relief, lowering my pinning blood pressure. I was surprised to find that despite the fact she had been feeling so ill and frightened the night before, this morning, here she was, getting herself up and to the bathroom all on her own. I crossed the room and knocked slightly on the other side of the bathroom door, restating my greeting from a little closer range, "Mom… I'm here."

"Hey guess what? An angel came to visit me last night!" She nonchalantly shot back through the door. Her tone was calm and matter-of-fact, as if she were stating the mail carrier had just dropped by to deliver her mail.

"What did you say?" I asked her, wondering if I had heard her right.

The door swung open, and there stood this little woman, my mom, wearing her hospital gown and a big smile. She continued with a chuckle to repeat herself, "An angel came to my room last night…" Then she added, "But I thought it was you."

I quickly reached for her arm to help her keep her balance as she made her way back to bed. She was in an amazing mood. Chipper and chatty, the opposite of what I was expecting to find that morning. She was awake, feeling good and ready to share all about the previous night's events that had happened there in her room.

"You saw an angel and you thought it was me?" I repeated it back to her as I didn't quite understand a word of what she'd just said.

"Yes, an angel came to my room last night. You know how afraid I was to be here in this hospital by myself? Well, when you left, I started praying that the Lord would comfort me. I was so scared of being all alone. I finally fell asleep, but then suddenly I woke up to what I thought was the back of your hand brushing my cheek. I thought to myself, *"Oh Teri Lynn is here. She came back to sit with me."* So, I opened my eyes expecting to see you. But instead, there was this bright light. It was so bright I had to shut my eyes and turn away from it. I didn't know what it was. I thought maybe the nurse had left a light on and it was shining right in my face. I tried to look again, but that light was so bright that I couldn't keep my eyes open. If I turned my face away, I could keep my eyes open longer. When I did that, I could see on the edge of my view that the bright light was an angel!"

She went on with her incredibly detailed story, "Oh, honey. He was so beautiful!" A look of precious awe spread across her face as she thought about the image she'd seen. Then she rephrased her comment, "Listen to me. I keep calling him a 'he.' I didn't think angels were male or female, but this one certainly did look male!" She then began motioning his size by lifting her arms high and wide, "He was sooooo tall and his shoulders were really wide. And that thing that you always hear about angel wings? That's not how it is!" By now she was on a roll, "You know how in pictures you always see angel's wings sticking straight out of their back? Well! It isn't like that at all!" Cupping her left hand over the rounded top of her right shoulder she continued to describe what she saw, "It's more like this," squeezing her shoulder. "His wings were part of him, part of his shoulders. He lifted and lowered them from here. He had folded them behind him, and they fit right in place, so smoothly. They were so beautiful!" There was that word again. Every other sentence was sprinkled with the adjective BEAUTIFUL. Her recollection was clear and concise.

Without my prompting, she went on to describe his clothing. "His clothes were a very bright white. There was a shimmery gold edge all the way around him. It surrounded him completely. He was there, right there next to my bed." She pointed to the space between the left side of her bed and the blank wall. "I had to keep closing my eyes every few seconds from the brightness. But every time I opened them again, he was still there! I felt like we'd known each other for years. But I didn't know who he was! Just having him there… I wasn't afraid anymore. I felt so much peace. Then I decided I was going to look straight at him, even if it hurt my eyes. So, I turned my face back in his direction with my eyes still closed. I thought I'll just open and close them once, really quick. But, when I opened them that time, he was gone!"

She then pondered her own story, "I wonder who he was and why he was here…" The answer to me seemed quite clear, "Mom, I think maybe he was your guardian angel." With that she replied without skipping a beat, "Oh good! I thought he might be the angel of death!" Her stark and matter-of-fact response cracked me up. Seriously? Only my mother…

Mom soon adjusted to her chemo treatments. She continued to hit one milestone after the next. She beat the six-month marker and then flew past a year. Her numbers were steadily improving. The doctor seemed a bit baffled. Our faith and hope grew with every good report. Much of the cancer was shrinking. Soon, two years came and went. Then three. My mom, despite the difficulties that were thrown her way, appeared to be winning this battle with cancer. She was holding steady in the fight. Finally, in the fourth year after her original diagnosis, the winds began to change. By this point, being on and off chemo many times, as well as personal challenges at home, mom was becoming weaker. Her numbers were changing— and not for the better. It seemed the cancer was getting the upper hand. Her life became increasingly difficult to manage. The culmination of it all was taking its staggering toll not only on her body, but now on her entire outlook as well. A shift in mom's prayers began. One afternoon, after a particularly distressing day, she confessed to me that she had stopped praying for God to heal her and had begun asking Him to simply take her *home*. I wasn't okay with this, by any means, but certainly, I understood why.

Even though it felt, to me, like mom was giving up, I couldn't say I blamed her. But being selfish, I wanted her here. I wanted a miracle. I wanted my mom. I didn't want to let her go. We'd seen so many hopeful signs unfold in those four years. Now I had to deal with the crumbling of them all.

Halfway through that fourth year, during a quiet summer evening, mom lost the fight for good. But she'd won her victory. Her prayer was answered. She finally went home to heaven. That evening as I sat next to her bedside, holding her hand as she took her last breath, I had peace. This was for the best. This was what mom wanted. To finally be with Jesus. To be in heaven with her Heavenly Father. Though I didn't want to say goodbye, this wasn't about me.

Dave was there in the room when she left us. Afterwards, he shared his comforting experience with me. Later, he would share it with those in attendance at her funeral service. He said that night, as we all gathered around her bed, saying our final goodbyes, he felt the unmistakable swoosh of a holy presence entering the room there with us. Then after she breathed that last breath, the presence left the room as well. We believe God's holy presence was there that night standing among us in that moment. HE had come to personally escort this precious one, His daughter, along the final path of her life's journey. Never again would my mom be alone.

Coming home that night was difficult yet I couldn't deny the peace that lingered. Sitting in the dark until the sun came up, I didn't want to sleep, even if I could have. This night was sacred. I missed mom already and was trying to take in the new normal that was beginning with the dawn. So much about the afterlife is unknown to us humans. It's times like these that we must cling to the faith we claim.

As tiny gleams of the morning rays sliced through the darkness of my living room, I was wrestling. I knew I should have plenty of faith to see this through, but I was feeling incredibly weak. In the hidden part of my heart, I secretly longed for God to show up once more. I wished for, but didn't dare ask for, a sign. I wanted some kind of assurance that mom had indeed made it to her destination. To heaven. I scolded myself for not having enough faith to just know it was true. After everything I had witnessed the past four years, why was I having trouble believing now? I reminded myself of my mother's unshakable faith in a God who always seemed to comfort her when she needed it most. Of all the encouraging dreams and scripture verses that came at just the right time throughout this whole ordeal. Of the angel that visited her in the hospital bed, just because she felt so alone. I reminded myself of that first day upon hearing the news; how could I forget her impressive talk with God, when she prayed, "Whether You decide to heal me or take me home, let this be used for Your glory." No. I would not ask for a sign now. What more did I need?

As the morning hours passed, my husband rose and came into the living room to join me. After grabbing a cup of coffee, he reached over the sink and slid the window open. A slight breeze made its way through the room. It felt like life. Though my heart was breaking, somehow the movement of this gentle wind gave me comfort. As we sat there in silence, a loud snap or smack sound caught our attention. My husband jumped up and went to the kitchen where the sound had come from. Over by the window, lying on the counter was one of the colored scripture verse cards from the tiny ceramic bread box my mom had given me. We concluded that the little gust of wind must have blown it from the windowsill. It was a popular place where we would leave those little cards, after pulling one. Someone must have placed this one there earlier. Picking it up and slapping it back down onto the counter, yes, that definitely was the sound we'd both just heard. Just then our son Zach walked into the kitchen. Dave turned to him and asked if he had been the one who'd placed the card in the windowsill.

Zach, looking at the card, replied, "Yes. I did that…" as he picked it up from the counter, to place it back among the others. "But I didn't do that!" he said as he pointed in the direction of the container. There in the little ceramic bread box, gathered among the others, a lone little scripture verse card, was raised up. It was sticking halfway above all the rest—right in the middle.

I jumped up and ran into the kitchen. All three of us stood around that little scripture verse container staring at this one ominous card, almost nervous to touch it. Slowly reaching toward it, I gently pulled it from the rest. Though I never asked for that confirmation, that final sign, God saw my breaking heart. He met me in my sorrow with the same comforting words mom had spoken to Him the day they'd had their talk about her cancer.

The little card read "… So now also, Christ shall be magnified in my body, whether it be by life or by death." (Philippians 1:20. KJV)

One more time… God met me in my mama.

# MY STORY

*Slowing Down to Pray & Reflect*

As I read Chapter Twelve, I was reminded of my own…

When I think about what I just wrote, it makes me feel…

I do / don't believe God performs miracles.

I have / haven't personally experienced anything I would call "a miracle from God."

I think believing in miracles is…

The person in my life with a faith I admire is / there is no person in my life with real faith.

If something happened in my life that someone else would call a miracle, I might call it…

I believe if something can't be explained that means / doesn't mean it could be a miracle.

I believe a person's "good behavior" has much / has little / has nothing to do with receiving a "sign from God."

The idea that God would actually "talk" to me personally, makes me feel…

A lie I have uncovered concerning miracles is…

# PRAYERS & MEDITATIONS

## *Chapter 12*

And he said, "Truly I tell you, unless you change and become like children, you will never enter the kingdom of heaven." Matthew 18:3 (NIV)

Therefore encourage one another and build each other up, just as in fact you are doing. 1Thessalonians 5:11 (NIV)

Have I not commanded you? Be strong and courageous. Do not be afraid, do not be discouraged, for the LORD your God will be with you wherever you go. Joshua 1:9 (NIV)

Wait for the LORD; be strong and take heart and wait for the LORD. Psalm 27:14 (NIV)

Let us think of ways to motivate one another to acts of love and good works. And let us not neglect our meeting together, as some people do, but encourage one another, especially now that the day of his return is drawing near. Hebrews 10:24-25. (NLT)

For I am the LORD your God who takes hold of your right hand and says to you, Do not fear; I will help you. Isaiah 41:13 (NIV)

Seek the LORD while he may be found, call on him while he is near. Isaiah 55:6 (NIV)

Peace I leave with you; my peace I give you. I do not give to you as the world gives. Do not let your hearts be troubled and do not be afraid. John 14:27 (NIV)

The righteous person may have many troubles, but the LORD delivers him from them all. Psalm 34:19-20 (NIV)

"I have told you these things, so that in me you may have peace. In this world you will have trouble. But take heart! I have overcome the world." John 16:33 (NIV)

My Prayer…

CONCLUSION

# MEETING GOD
# IN YOUR STORY

*G*od has planted Himself all around us. Our inability to see or recognize Him doesn't negate the validity of His existence. His words, the written scripture, share His heart. Creation itself reflects His beauty. If we'll simply *look*, we'll be unable to deny His fingerprints everywhere. All that surrounds us—ALL OF IT—was made with one thought in mind: to gently point us back to Him. He wants us to know our Creator. How is it that we so easily miss it? Miss *Him*?

We have everything we need to recognize and acknowledge His truth. Sadly, instead, we turn away. We shut our eyes tightly to what's in front of us and plug our ears to what's behind. Why? Why would we do this? The reason might be, we don't want to be wrong. More simply put, we can't *afford* to be wrong. There's too much at stake. Our pride is much too valuable.

If we step out toward Him, in our wobbly unfamiliar faith, then find the crossing bridge suddenly disappearing, what then? Turning ourselves and our circumstances over to this mysterious Heavenly Being only to wind up alone and embarrassed is not a risk we're willing to take. What a spectacle we'd make of ourselves should our lives unexplainably turn upside down after declaring some Divine protection or intervention from it all. Degrading humiliation would certainly follow. What would be thought of us then? Therefore, we are determined to never let that happen. Just the mere entertaining of the idea seems the farthest thing from rational. We'll stay right here, thank you, in the safety of our human-built comforts and our stained-glass fortresses, at the detriment of our very souls. Sitting in our fear demands payment of the highest price. It ultimately costs us *everything*. Living this way, we're merely a shadow of ourselves. Our true identities remain hidden, untapped. Sadly, our God-given potential, our true purpose on this planet never sees the light of day. Who we really are is never given the opportunity to manifest.

When we pacify the innate longing inside ourselves by creating a pliable God, made in our own image, we've inadvertently chosen to travel a destructively hybrid path. It seems right in theory, but out of fear and arrogance, we've traded places with Him. We become the creator and He, the created. In our efforts to control, we've distorted Him, fashioning a God to our own liking.

As we've discussed in this humble book, our versions of God are many, springing up like countless weeds in a vinedresser's choicest field. Yet, with all these roads traveled, why are we still at a loss when it comes to knowing God? Why have none of these paths ever taken us where we originally intended to go? Along the way, sure, there were times we thought we were close, but in the end, we never quite got there. None of these aberrations ever lead to satisfaction.

With hundreds of world-wide religions, and the renegade versions we've made up in our heads; none quite fill the hole in us. We can't seem to feed this insatiable hunger to know this living God.

The beautiful truth is; no matter how many warped images we've held up to the sky, He remains unchanged. This God is not altered by our efforts to mold Him. Unsmudged by the touch of our dirtiest human hands, He stands in the complete perfection of His unfailing love for us. He is who He is, despite our inability to see Him as such. He knows and understands we're made of the soil from this planet, and we come with our share of grime-covered baggage. And guess what? He's ready and willing to meet us right in the messy middle of it all.

The question is, and has always been: "Are we?" Really?

When will we stop trying to manhandle God? When will we stop looking for Him in the dusty corners of our man-made buildings? He's not hiding from us under some dark and pointy religious umbrella. Nor is He sleeping under a numbing wooden pew. Sadly, striving to find Him on our own, or through a religious ritual has inadvertently dulled any passion we may have had and has only served to confuse us more. No wonder so many of us have discouragingly given up. After all our searching we can't help but believe either He doesn't exist, or He's hidden Himself in the ominous clouds above. We conclude if He's there, He must be so far away that He'll never hear the tender breaking of our lonely hearts. With this sad thought, we finally give up. We'll never know He's always been as close as the whisper from the humble lips that faced His direction.

If we can stop chasing the madness, and running from our fears, we'll finally find what our souls have been searching for: We will meet God. He will show up. It's a promise. It just might not look the way we thought it would. For our own good, He's not interested in sharing the stage. Relabeled and regurgitated wisdom may sound impressive at first, but it's far from organic, and leads to separation from the original source. THE truth our hearts instinctively know and recognize, the bedrock of our true existence, can't be peddled. It can't be sold, and it can't be bought. It is and has always remained *a gift*. This gift doesn't change with time. It's not designed to tickle our ears or to simply make us happy; no. It's not that superficial. This gift is *extremely personal*.

As humans living on a quite imperfect planet, we see chaos and pain on a daily basis. If we're lucky, we've carved out a reasonable existence, with a few threads of happiness woven through our otherwise turbulent lives. If we've managed to grab hold of even a fraction of what we've strived for professionally or personally, we feel as though we should be grateful. And maybe we should. But still, underneath it all we chastise ourselves. We tend to feel the gnawing tug of guilt, because nothing we've managed to achieve or accumulate seems to satisfy us *completely,* does it?

We can reach the pinnacle of everything we thought we wanted, only to find once we have it in our hand, the letdown eventually comes. From each mountaintop's view we wonder, "Is this all there is to this life?" We've invested our most precious commodity—our time—in an attempt to satisfy our deep longing only to find it never lasts. The demand for more always returns.

Always.

When will our comfort finally last? It seems no matter how we've tried, we cannot avoid the pain. We shake a fist at this God who refuses to take the suffering from our shoulders, from our world. Dare we consider this God a selfish jerk? A cruel tyrant? Thoughts like this make us bitter. We cinch our armor snugly around ourselves for our own self-protection. We don't need this unreliable God. In our efforts to numb our own pain, we wall ourselves off from Him.

It's guaranteed in this life, that each of us will have our share of troubles. No matter who we are, no matter our pay scale or where we were born, there's no escaping this fact for any one of us. We all experience our storms. When the hurricanes hit us, unless we're made of stone, we can't help but become undone. Of course, we pray for the adversity to pass us by—to be taken from us—for the threat to be lifted and the sun to shine again. In those moments, we sense our own helplessness. Our own hated weakness. What we thought would save us has instead left us with nothing more than overwhelming grief. In our storm, we have missed Him. Through all the rain, we couldn't see Him standing right there. He has always been with us. He longed to comfort us in our devastation but we couldn't (or wouldn't) hear Him, as we focused on our pain.

This planet is tragically broken. Because we live on it, we will be affected by the pain of that fact. Because man has been given free will, this planet will always suffer as a result. God will not remove man's free will, but He promises to comfort us in its fallout. He wants to hold our hand and walk us through the scariest, darkest, ugliest places we know—even the places we've nailed shut and barricaded ourselves away from.

We cannot truly know Him until we're finally willing to unlock the door. The lock has always been on the inside, on our side, not His.

When we're hurting or afraid, instead of cowering behind our fortress walls, begging God to remove what threatens us, can we, instead, open the door and reach for His hand? Even in the blackest of nights, we can tighten our grip in His. It's in these moments we embrace the opportunity to witness a new strength rise in us—a strength we've never possessed on our own. This Supernatural ability enables us to stand and not run. No longer must we hide, trying to protect ourselves. No more frantically grabbing at what's closest, pulling it over our own heads. Hand in hand with His unshakable truth, we can know *we will be okay*. He has us. He loves us. And no matter what it looks like now, the big picture remains sure—He is fiercely protective of us! Whatever may come at us, trying to rob what little faith we have left, it will ultimately have to answer to Him. Even though what's happening may be terrible in the moment, it won't be wasted. He promises to somehow turn it into good, for us and for others. Armed with this knowledge, we can unshakably know our God is indeed greater than anything. In the times we are the weakest, He is exceedingly and overwhelmingly strong.

Once we embrace this truth, we will see there's truly nothing we can't face when we are standing in His strength. We also begin to realize that if there were never any obstacles, we would never know the reality of this truth. All this time, as we begged God to deliver us from our problems, we never realized the treasure hidden inside those hard moments. Every day brings its share of troubles, the invitation continually awaits. We will be the ones to decide what we do with it.

Each of us has a story. The story can be extraordinarily rich with hope or plungingly deep with despair, or at times, both. It will be a matter of who we've allowed to hold the pen during the chapters when the waters have turned rough. It's our free will, and has always been our choice. We can see our problems and disappointments as God abandoning us when we needed Him most; but dare we consider it has been us doing the abandoning? We have abandoned our faith in Him when our skies turn their darkest. When things didn't turn out the way we'd planned, we are the ones who chose to resent Him. Have we gotten so wise on our own as to think that we know more than He does? Honestly, sometimes, yes. What else can explain the ambivalence we harbor toward Him during and long after these difficult times.

What will you choose to do now?

As we near the end of our journey together, through these pages, I hope you've taken the time to write down your thoughts, your fears, and your prayers within each chapter. As I mentioned earlier, as I wrote the words of this book, I prayed all along for those who would eventually be reading it. I've been thinking of *you*. My prayer has been that God would reveal the lies that have held you back so long. That the false beliefs others have cloaked over your eyes would begin to fall away. That He would reveal Himself to you in ways you've never experienced before. My prayer mostly has been that when you set down this book, you will take with you an encouraged heart and new mindset. That instead of running from, you will begin looking to Him to give you the strength to stand and face your hardest moments. My prayer is that you will break free from what has so long held you captive; your past; what you're dealing with right now; or even as you look ahead to your future. May you now be filled with a new boldness because of Him and His love for you. I hope you re-read your journaling in between these pages time and again, growing more each time you do. I've prayed that He will continue revealing and reshaping His truths in you, about you, and for you and that you may truly grab hold of it.

There's a blueprint, a statement of this truth written for our comfort and for our knowledge: Scribed long ago are the words from Psalm 139:16, *"Your eyes saw my unformed body; all the days ordained for me were written in your book before one of them came to be"* (NIV).

For every person who's had a beating heart, there's always been a unique story carved in time that was meant just for them. This very personal memoir was conceived forever in advance, before we ever came to be. The idea of *you* had been dancing inside Him long before you took your first breath. Before you took your first steps, He was there, already gently holding you up. You've only begun hearing the Divine music that's been circling around you all along.

If the words are still vague and the melody too faint, don't worry. Your inability to hear the music doesn't negate its playing. Not at all. Simply tighten your grasp. Don't pull your hand from His. Keep going. It's baby steps. Your ears will attune, and the words will rise in you soon enough.

I now excitedly pass the baton to you. Along with it comes a challenge. Are you willing to continue expanding your heart to allow a foolish notion its rightful place? The childlike thought that you still don't know as much as you thought you did, and that it's okay. Our own reasoning or wanting to explain away the why's of our lives can be our biggest obstacles when it comes to deepening our relationship with God. He certainly gets blamed a lot for things He never said or never did. He's misunderstood so often. No wonder we can't see Him or embrace Him when we need Him most. We've been busy pointing our fingers out of our own silly pride. We don't know everything. That was never the plan. If we'll continue to simply focus on the One who does, we'll finally find that elusive rest our weary souls have longed for. We need to trust the process.

That's why He gave us His word. He put it in writing, and you can take that writing to the bank—because it's gold. Whatever you've previously thought about the Bible, I'm praying that you will now see it with fresh eyes. It's never been just a book to be read from cover to cover and then placed back on the shelf. It's not a collection of writings to muse over or to brag about memorizing. My prayer is that you begin to see scripture simply as it is, a beautifully written love letter. This is a letter, written *to you personally,* as well as to all of us. We are His creation. Through His written word, He speaks to us as a whole, yet also whispers the most personal comforts to each one individually. His word is alive, living and breathing. It fills our lungs as well. We will suffocate without it.

I'm so proud of your bravery for taking this step, being willing to pick up, read and finish this book. In the honesty you've shared here—facing your fears and giving God your prayers and journaling, this book has now become your own. Your story is incredible, and the best part is you've just begun to fill the pages!

We all have.

May you grow in your understanding of how very faithful God has been and will continue to be as He meets you *the hard way*.

# BONUS FEATURE

## *My Choices*

What I choose to focus on affects my moods.

My moods affect the actions I choose.

The actions I choose affect my day.

My days become my years.

My years become my life.

My choices matter.

I choose.

I can choose to keep God out of my life.
I can choose to deny God hears my prayers.
I can choose to find and call out the bad in my situations.
I can choose to turn negative emotions into worry.
I can choose to lose my faith during the storms.
I can choose to handle my worries on my own.
I can choose to believe I control my own life.
I can choose to decide my own path without asking for help.
I can choose to follow my own voice.
I can choose to focus on the painful and unfair
situations in my life.
I can choose to dwell on my own thoughts and expectations.
I can choose to focus on the faults in others.
I can choose to hold grudges and vow to remember
the pain they caused.
I can choose to expect nothing good will happen
because I don't see it.
I can choose to dwell on and expand toxic thoughts when they hit.
I can choose to make judgments of others and
take revenge as I see fit.
I can choose to retaliate.
I can choose self-promotion and arrogance.
I can choose to be impatient and demanding.
I can refuse to care, help or give of my time for others.
I can see my negative situations as punishment,
failures or time wasted.
I can choose selfishness.
I can choose to quit.
I can choose to harden my heart toward others and even myself.
I can choose despair.
I can choose hatred, jealousy and envy.
I can choose fate.

I can choose to let God into my life.

I can choose to believe God hears me when I pray.

I can choose to find and call out the good in my situations.

I can choose to turn negative emotions into prayers.

I can choose to hold onto faith during the storms.

I can choose to give my worries to God.

I can choose to trust God is in control.

I can choose to ask God to direct my steps.

I can choose to listen for His voice.

I can choose to keep my focus on the good things,
the blessings in my life.

I can choose to remind myself of God's word and
His promises to me.

I can choose to believe the best in others.

I can choose to forgive; even when it still hurts.

I can choose to believe good will happen, even before I see it.

I can choose to unplug and dump toxic thoughts when they hit.

I can choose to leave the judgements to the only
One who knows the truth.

I can choose to be merciful, remembering when
I have received it also.

I can choose humility.

I can choose patience.

I can choose compassion.

I can choose to see my negative situation as
a positive learning tool.

I can choose gratitude.

I can choose to get back up.

I can choose to keep my heart open and tender.

I can choose hope.

I can choose love.

I can choose God.

# ABOUT THE AUTHOR

*T*eri Brinsley is the founder and CEO of Waterfall, an organization she created to bring encouragement to the weary soul. **Her inspiring true stories have been featured on Oprah, Larry King, It's a Miracle, and KFIA radio.**

She's a contributing writer in the published books Heavenly Miracles and The Miracle of Sons.

She's been married for over thirty years to her handsome husband David. Together they've raised four children and have added two bonus sons when their daughters married.

Five of the cutest grandkids on the planet call her Nana. David and Teri reside in El Dorado Hills, CA. (You can find out more about Teri at TeriBrinsleyWrites.com or visit her inspirational website at Waterfalllive.com.)